GOLDEN BOY

THE RISE AND RISE OF HARRY KANE

By Andy Greeves

SJH PUBLISHING

First edition

Published by SJH Publishing

298 Regents Park Road, London N3 2SZ

020 8371 4000

sjhpublishing.org

ISBN: 978-1-782818-16-8

Printed and bound in the UK by CPI Books.

**IN MEMORY OF
TOBY DAVID HOTSPUR GREEVES**
5-28 AUGUST 2014

Andy Greeves is a freelance football writer who has contributed to the official matchday programmes of Tottenham Hotspur FC and The Football Association as well as *FourFourTwo*, *When Saturday Comes*, *The Guardian* and the *Tottenham and Wood Green Journal*. A lifelong Spurs supporter and season ticket holder, Andy has witnessed the rise and rise of English football's golden boy, Harry Kane, first-hand. Follow @AndyGreeves on Twitter.

CONTENTS

ACKNOWLEDGEMENTS

I would first of all like to thank Jules Gammond and G2 Entertainment for approaching me with the opportunity to write this book. As a life-long Spurs supporter and a season ticket holder, it gives me particular delight that the topic of my first biography should be Harry Kane – an individual who I have gained so much pleasure in watching score goal after goal for my beloved Tottenham Hotspur in recent years!

Also, a massive thank you to each and every person who took the time to speak to me during the process of writing this book. To Les Ferdinand MBE – an ex-England international of course and Harry's former coach at Spurs, who has provided such a lovely foreword for this title. To Harry Redknapp and Chris Ramsey, who offered insight into Harry's early days at White Hart Lane. And to Daniel Wynne, who has described every Harry Kane goal for Tottenham in his role as club commentator! Thanks too to Rob Mason – a good friend of mine and a former editor at Sunderland AFC, who I worked with in my day-to-day role as a freelance writer for a number of football club matchday programmes – who helped make this all possible!

Thank you to those who offered their thoughts on Harry's exploits away from N17 too. To Paul Levy, Steve Nassbaum, Ted Herring, George Lampey and Robert Tanner, who covered his loan moves at the likes of Leyton Orient, Millwall, Norwich City and Leicester City. To the England fans – Mark Heelis, Joe Lo, Matt Stewart, Charlie Brown and Anthony Wall – who watched Harry in action at the 2018 FIFA World Cup and gave their verdict on a memorable tournament. To Spurs podcasters Mike Leigh and Richard 'Crackers' Cracknell. And not forgetting Harry Kane lookalike Paul Foden.

A final big thank you to my beautiful wife Cathryn and my son, Henry Jon Hotspur Greeves, who have been so supportive in everything I do. Likewise, my mother Janet and father John Greeves, who from being nicknamed 'Greevsie' in homage to Jimmy Greaves (different surname spellings noted!) in a London comprehensive school back in 1960s so began our family love affair with Spurs. Thanks to my mother-in-law Lynne and Team Toby for keeping Henry entertained while 'Daddy' has been writing!

I have written this book in the memory of my other son, Toby David Hotspur Greeves, who passed away in August 2014, aged just 23 days. Toby was my 'golden boy', who I miss dearly. I dreamt of taking him to a Spurs match one day and while it never got to happen in person, I've got no doubt he's at each and every game with me in spirit. When the rainbow shone over the East Stand after Tottenham's final match at White Hart Lane against Manchester United in May 2017, I'm convinced Toby was watching on from 'The Shelf' on the clouds.

ANDY GREEVES, AUGUST 2018

@ANDYGREEVES

FOREWORD

BY LES FERDINAND MBE

I've said it time and time again. If I'd told you five or six years ago that Harry Kane would achieve the things he has in his career by the age of 25 – a Premier League superstar, England's captain and the World Cup Golden Boot winner – I would have been lying. That's not to say Tim Sherwood, Chris Ramsey and I – who coached Harry in Tottenham's academy and later at first-team level – didn't see the potential. I remember watching Harry in training one day, striking the ball as sweetly with his left foot as he did with his right and thinking 'the kid's got something'.

Like Harry, Tottenham Hotspur are my boyhood club and I was fortunate enough to play nearly 150 matches for Spurs between 1997 to 2003. I returned to White Hart Lane in 2008 to help coach the team's strikers, working specifically with players in the under-21 squad. I remember coming across Harry for the first time – he instantly struck me as a good kid. He was keen to learn, keen to develop the skills and mindset required to become a professional footballer.

We had a great group of youngsters at the club at that time. Those players fed off one another in terms of their attitude and how they pushed each other on. They challenged each other and us as coaches to help them become the very best players they could be. In my early days back at Spurs, it was players like Ryan Mason, Tom Carroll and Dean Parrott that we were talking about as having the ability to go on and do fantastic things. We felt that Harry would have a decent career but I guess the question back then was, would that career be in the Premier League?

I worked a lot with Harry on both his finishing and positioning. While I was at the club Tim, Chris and I analysed each under-21s match. I would say what I'd seen from a centre-forward's point of view and I'd identify ways in which each striker could make improvements. We'd then go off and discuss our findings with the players. We worked on aspects of the players' game, often in individual groups – Tim with the midfielders for example, myself with the strikers etc.

One of the big things with Harry was encouraging him to get his shot off earlier. We see it time and time again in football – strikers getting in good positions to score, but they might not hit the ball because there is a defender nearby for example. Some strikers are always looking for that 'perfect shot'. The thing is, the perfect shot for me is the one that ends up in the back of the net. It doesn't have be the curling effort into the top corner from the edge of the area. I'd often tell Harry not to be afraid of shooting through players legs when the goalkeeper might be unsighted or there might be a deflection. The bread and butter for any centre-forward is getting in that 18-yard-box and finishing. For me, there are few better at that than Harry in world football right now… right foot, left foot, heading… he's got the lot.

Harry's journey to becoming a first-team regular at Spurs was a lengthy one. He had two good loan spells at Leyton Orient and Millwall followed by the disappointment at Norwich City of breaking a bone in his foot in just his second match for the Canaries. Then there was a fourth loan, to another of my former clubs – Leicester City. It didn't really work out for Harry at the King Power Stadium and Foxes' supporters that watched him back then never really got to see the potential we saw during the same period on the training pitches at Spurs.

When Harry returned to Tottenham from that loan spell at Leicester, it was like something triggered in him. He was always a hard worker but he started doing even more. It wasn't just out on the training pitch but also in the gym, as he honed his physique. When he was in the under-21s, Harry carried a bit of puppy fat. But soon after his time at Leicester, we started to see a real athlete emerging.

Harry made his Spurs debut back in 2010 in the Europa League, but he only had a handful of matches in the first-team thereafter before he was sent out on those various loans. By the time Tim, Chris and I assumed first-team responsibilities at Spurs in December 2013, 'H' was chomping at the bit to be selected once again. He had reached a level of confidence I think most centre-forwards do when you think 'I'm ready to play, I know what I can do'.

Harry was on fire in the under-21s and in training too, but manager Tim Sherwood still showed a lot of courage giving him his first Premier League start for Spurs against Sunderland in April 2013. Even though Roberto Soldado struggled in front of goal in his debut season, the Tottenham fans really seemed to warm to the Spaniard, who Harry was affectively replacing up front.

Harry quickly repaid Tim's faith, scoring against Sunderland and also in his next two Premier League games. He started the last six matches in succession at the end of the 2013-14 season prior to Tim, Chris and I leaving Spurs. In hindsight, given how well he's done, I often wonder if we could have started Harry in the first-team even earlier? To be honest though, it doesn't really matter now where or when his breakthrough came. The important thing is that when he took to the White Hart Lane pitch in April 2013, it was Harry's time.

Under Tim's replacement, Mauricio Pochettino, H has continued to flourish. While I'm not saying he's better than these players yet, in Harry I see the intelligence of movement that Teddy Sheringham used to have and the finishing ability of Alan Shearer. On the topic of Shearer, if Harry can avoid any major injuries during his career, I think he has as good a chance of any striker around right now of breaking Alan's all-time Premier League goal scoring record.

I thought Harry did an excellent job for England as captain at the recent World Cup and to score six goals at the tournament was an incredible achievement. The future looks so bright for him and from a club perspective, Spurs fans will be hoping he stays with his boyhood team for the rest of his career. Harry is clearly driven by goal scoring statistics – like any forward worth their weight in salt – and the ultimate record to break at Tottenham would be Jimmy Greaves' all-time scoring record.

I can only echo the nice things you read and hear about Harry – he is as fantastic a human being as he is a footballer. He has gone on to surpass all my expectations and my hope is he can carry on the rich vein of form he's show pretty much from his first Premier League start for Spurs. The incredible thing is, I still think there's a lot more to come from him. For Tottenham Hotspur and England supporters, that really is a tantalising prospect!

LES FERDINAND MBE - AUGUST 2018

*Les donated his fee for this foreword to Prostate Cancer UK (prostatecanceruk.org)

INTRODUCTION

As Harry Kane flashed a shot wide of Thibaut Courtois' goal during England's third place play-off defeat to Belgium at the World Cup, the striker had a rueful look on this face. The lad from Chingford, who has made a career out of scoring goals, had been expecting to see the net bulge when the ball left his right foot. After a moment of reflection in response to his miscue, he wiped his brow, picked himself up off his knees and got on with the game.

Such calmness and steely determination in the face of a setback has long been a Harry Kane trait. It has got him to a place in his career where former Ballon d'Or winner Zinedine Zidane considers him a 'complete player'. It has enabled him to make it into the first-team and become a legend at his favourite boyhood club, Tottenham Hotspur. And it led him to captaining his country to the semi-final of Russia 2018, where he won the Golden Boot.

Growing up in north east London, Kane showed early promise with a ball at his feet. He scored for fun for his local team, Ridgeway Rovers and for his Chingford school side. But a series of rejections – including his release by Arsenal as an eight-year-old – suggested he would be one of the many that would try and ultimately fail in their mission of becoming a professional footballer.

He was handed a second chance at Spurs and rose through the academy ranks. But his path to the first-team was thwarted on more than one occasion, as the club opted to bring in a new multi-million-pound signing. He was loaned to Leyton Orient, to Millwall, to Norwich City. He was loaned to Leicester City too where he spent much of his time at the then-Championship club wondering 'if I can't make it here, how am I ever going to make it at White Hart Lane?'

But make it he did. His hours of dedication on the training field paid off. His goals and overall momentum became such that he couldn't be left on the side-lines any longer. With a maturity belying his years, he rose to become the professional Spurs fans were proud to call 'one of their own' and the golden boy a nation would one day pin their World Cup hopes and dreams on.

There have continued to be disappointments along the way. Injuries, missed chances and the ultimately unsuccessful Premier League title charges. Not to mention the goalless Augusts. But from each of those knockbacks has risen a player who refuses to be beat. The back-to-back Premier League Golden Boot recipient, the hat-trick hero, the last-minute match winner, the national team captain.

Kane's standing in the global game at the age of 25 is such that he could command a starting role in any team on the globe. Perhaps the biggest club side of them all – Real Madrid – have made no secret of the fact they'd love Harry to fill their famous Los Blancos kit. But his decision to remain loyal to his first footballing love, Spurs, speaks volumes for the individual. He is a throwback to a more romantic time in football's past, where players were grateful to represent their club not the other way around. A time when 'one-club men' were the norm not the exception.

If his journey hadn't been as tough and uncertain as it was at times for Harry, one wonders if he'd be half the player? It's doubtful he'd be half the man. It's the adversity that spurs him on and provides the substance for the humble, driven individual we see before us.

CHAPTER ONE

CAPTAIN'S DUTY

Shortly after the draw for the 2018 FIFA World Cup was made in Moscow, former England captain Alan Shearer perhaps summed up the expectations of a nation ahead of the tournament: "England won't win (the) World Cup but (the) draw gives us chance to improve," wrote the Newcastle United legend in a BBC Sport article, adding a cautionary tale: "Let's not get carried away – we have been here plenty of times before… history tells us that things can go horribly wrong."

England were paired with Belgium in Group G at the draw for Russia 2018. Roberto Martinez's 'Red Devils' were ranked as the fifth-best national team in the world at that time – some ten places higher than Gareth Southgate's Three Lions. With Tunisia (ranked 27th) and Panama (ranked 56th) making up the four-team group though, it seemed – on paper at least – that England had been handed a favourable draw, especially when you consider Group F for example contained the likes of Germany, Mexico, South Korea and Sweden.

The 32 tournament teams were divided up into four pots prior to the draw, based on their FIFA World Rankings as of October 2017. A team from each pot was drawn to make up the eight groups. England were included amongst the second-ranked nations in pot 2 along with Spain, Peru, Switzerland, Colombia, Mexico, Uruguay and Croatia and as a result, they couldn't face any of those opponents in the group stage. There was also a restriction on no more than two European nations being in a single group.

Southgate acknowledged the draw could have been far tougher for England and commented that he "wasn't disappointed" to be missing out on facing five-time competition winners and top seeds Brazil in the group phase. He also said he was pleased to steer clear of Serbia – who were amongst the eight lowest ranked nations in pot four.

"What's exciting for our team is, although we lack some big match experience and we don't have at the moment trophies and medals on the table for a lot of the lads, I think that's all ahead for them and what's possible is exciting," Southgate told Sky Sports after the draw. "For me, it reminds me of one of the best days of my life, really, playing in my first game in a World Cup (against Tunisia in Marseille at France '98). The colour and vibrancy of that occasion and winning. To now have the chance to lead my country into that same game, same fixture, first game of the World Cup, is something I'm hugely proud of."

"Because we are second seeds, we have to have two games (against Tunisia and Panama) where we will be favourites and we have got to handle that. My experience of tournaments is that you usually have to get results in all three matches to go through the group and the objective is to qualify from the group."

With the thoughts of the Three Lions' damaging defeat to Iceland in the round of 16 at UEFA Euro 2016 still fresh in the memories of supporters, few were taking anything for granted ahead of Russia 2018. Southgate acknowledged the underwhelming results and performances of England at recent tournaments at the draw ceremony and commented: "In the last two tournaments we went out to teams we thought we'd beat." Quizzed on a potential quarter final meeting with Brazil or Germany in Russia, he added; "I'm not looking that far ahead".

Despite the let downs endured by England supporters in recent times, journalist Joe Lo – who attended the Three Lions' group matches with Tunisia and Panama in Russia – was in an optimistic mood ahead of the tournament,

"When the draw was made, I was delighted," he said. "I'd worked out England's dream draw beforehand and Panama and Tunisia were the worst third and fourth seeded teams we could play in my uninformed opinion! I knew Belgium were a good team but like England, they hadn't really performed to their full potential. I thought we'd probably – but not certainly – lose to them and finish second in our group.

"Before every tournament, I get over-excited and think England can win it. This enthusiasm was only partially balanced out by my memories of watching England lose to Iceland two years earlier. My perceived wisdom on the draw was that England would come second in the group and have a 50/50 chance against Colombia, Poland or Senegal before getting knocked out in the quarters. As I told the Reuters cameras after the Tunisia game, I thought England would get to the quarters and go out to Brazil or Germany. That was par for me and I'd have taken it."

If any player in the country had the ability to rouse belief in England's World Cup chances, it was of course Harry Kane. In qualification for Russia, the Walthamstow-born striker scored five times in seven appearances for the Three Lions, who topped their group with eight wins and two draws in their ten matches. 2017-18 proved to be Kane's most prolific season for his club Tottenham Hotspur to date, as he netted 41 times in 48 appearances for them in all competitions. In October 2017, he was the only Englishman to be included on the 30-player Ballon d'Or shortlist and was subsequently named as the tenth-best player in the world.

With his own thoughts occupied by club rather than national commitments at the time of the draw, Harry offered little public reaction, other than a Tweet that read;

"Belgium, Tunisia and Panama! Very excited for the #WorldCup and facing @JanVertonghen, @AlderweireldTob and @mousadembele #WorldCupDraw"

In 2017, Kane scored seven times in six appearances for England, winning senior caps numbers 18 to 23 in the process. His impressive haul of international goals that year began at Hampden Park, where he captained his country for the first time. He marked the occasion with a right-footed volley that gave the Three Lions a dramatic 93rd-minute equaliser in a 2-2 draw with Scotland in a World Cup qualifier. Two free-kicks from Leigh Griffiths on 87 and 90 minutes looked to have given the home side all three points. But Harry had other ideas and he was in the right place at the right time once again to slot home in the dying seconds of a game.

Three days later – and again wearing the captain's armband – Kane bagged a brace in England's 3-2 friendly defeat to France in Saint-Denis. He gave Gareth Southgate's side a ninth-minute lead, turning a Ryan Bertrand cross past his Spurs teammate and goalkeeper Hugo Lloris at the far post. Strikes from Samuel Umtiti and Djibril Sidibe saw the home side go in 2-1 up at half-time. A collision between Raphael Varane and Dele Alli in the French penalty area shortly after the break saw referee Davide Massa point to the spot and show Varane a red card. Harry coolly converted the resulting spot-kick but Ousmane Dembele won it for France late-on, on the same night a certain 18-year-old Monaco striker – Kylian Mbappe – tormented England's defence.

There were two more goals for Harry in a comfortable 4-0 win for the Three Lions in Malta on September 1, 2017. Three days later, Slovakia became the only international team to stop Kane scoring that year but the visitors still went down to a 2-1 defeat to Southgate's team at Wembley Stadium. Jordan Henderson skippered England against Malta and Slovakia but Kane resumed captain's duties for the final World Cup qualifiers with Slovenia and Lithuania.

On October 5, 2017, Kane led his England teammates out at Wembley – where he was playing his home matches for Spurs during the 2017-18 season – to face Slovenia. The Three Lions managed just five efforts on target during the game and had to wait until the fourth minute of stoppage time at the end of the game to break the deadlock when – surprise, surprise – Kane got the goal that sealed the nation's qualification for the World Cup.

"It wasn't an amazing performance but look, the most important thing was getting the win and qualifying for the World Cup," Kane told BBC Sport after the match. "We should be proud as a team, as a nation. We should all be enjoying tonight."

Kane's goal scoring run continued in Lithuania, as he got the only goal of the game. England completed their qualifying fixtures without experiencing a defeat and having secured 26 points from a possible 30 in topping Group F. The Tottenham striker subsequently missed England's friendly matches with Germany and Brazil, withdrawing from the squad through injury. He was rewarded for his efforts at international level, winning the 2017 England Men's Player of the Year award, polling 75% of the votes from members of the England Supporters' Club in the process.

Fast-forward to May 2018, Kane was named in Gareth Southgate's 23-man squad for Russia and shortly after, it was announced he would be the Three Lions' captain. In the weeks leading up to the tournament, Kane revealed that Southgate had earmarked him for that role during a squad meet-up at the Grove Hotel in Hertfordshire in March that year.

"We were talking for an hour or so and he said he wanted me to be the captain," said Kane in a St George's Park press conference. "I've had to keep it quiet a while but it's fantastic. I filled up with pride (upon hearing the news). I didn't tell anyone, except my fiancée, mum and dad, and brother. I had to keep my lips sealed."

At that same press conference, Southgate hailed Kane's "outstanding personal qualities".

"He is a meticulous professional and one of the most important things for a captain is that they set the standard every day. He has belief and high standards and it is a great message for the team to have a captain who has shown that it is possible to be one of the best in the world over a consistent period of time and that has been his drive.

"My feeling is that over the last 18 months in the camps that he's been with us he has shown that he has got the desire to take that into a team environment and he recognises the importance of bringing others with him.

"Of course, Harry will need the support of the other good leaders that we have got around him. You don't become a top team by just having a good captain with good values because that has got to spread right throughout the group but I think he is the one who is ready to take that challenge on."

Southgate and Kane spoke to the media on the same day the squad met for the first time ahead of two World Cup warm-up matches against Nigeria and Costa Rica. It was then the captain publicly stated his belief that the Three Lions could triumph in Russia.

"I believe we can (win the World Cup)," he said "I can't sit here and say we're not going to win it because we could do. It's just my mindset. I want to win at everything I do and I know a lot of players in the team want to win at everything they do."

The bookmakers were offering little backing to Harry's claims though. Pre-tournament odds for England to lift the trophy were 14/1 while Kane was a 16/1 shot for the Golden Boot. The relatively low levels of expectation amongst England supporters were perhaps reflected by the 20,000 or so empty seats when England took on Nigeria at Wembley Stadium on June 2.

The starting line-up that day included nine of the eleven players that featured from the kick-off against Tunisia in the Three Lions' opening World Cup game. Gary Cahill gave England an early lead before Kane continued his incredible scoring run at international level six minutes before the break. Harry's 18-yard effort, that slipped past Nigeria goalkeeper Francis Uzoho, was his eighth strike in his last seven England appearances. The Tottenham striker was substituted on 73 minutes and left the pitch to a standing ovation in the 2-1 victory.

Preparations for the tournament continued at Leeds United's Elland Road as England beat Costa Rica 2-0 thanks to goals from Marcus Rashford and Danny Welbeck. Kane was an unused substitute in the game that saw the squad's more peripheral members in action.

On June 12, the England squad flew to St Petersburg in their 62-seater, Boeing B757-200 private jet. Before take-off, the players and coaching staff posed for a team photograph in their £264, 3-piece Marks & Spencer suits. Skipper Kane sat in the front row with Southgate to his left and strike partner Raheem Sterling to his right. Touching down in Russia early that evening, the travelling party embarked on a 40-minute coach journey to their accommodation for the World Cup – the ForRestMix Club Hotel, Repino.

Images of the squad playing darts with the media at their training camp became commonplace for fans watching back at home. A fan of tungsten himself, Kane beat *Daily Mirror* journalist Andy Dunn with his final throw ahead of the team facing Colombia in the quarter finals. The players also spent their downtime ten-pin bowling and tuning into ITV2 series *Love Island*. Not Jamie Vardy mind, who announced he "can't stand" the show during the tournament. Speaking to BBC presenter Gabby Logan, Kane revealed that playing the video game *Fortnite* had helped him and his teammates "pass the time quite well" in Repino too.

"There are quite a few of us playing a few games of that," added Kane. "The missus is going to have a bit of a shock when I get home. She says it feels like we are on a boys' holiday – with everyone playing *Fortnite* and no babies. Stuff like that. We have got to enjoy it while it lasts." Away from the darts board and computer screens, England training sessions took place at the modest Stadium Spartak Zelenogorsk– a picturesque, 10km coastal drive away from the hotel.

Before the first training session in Russia, England manager

Gareth Southgate and skipper Kane were presented with some gifts from locals. The pair were handed a Russian samovar container – which is said to symbolise hospitality – and a loaf of salted bread by two women in national dress.

The World Cup kicked off on June 14 with hosts Russia thrashing Saudi Arabia 5-0 in the opening match of the tournament. Kane and England had to wait four days before their opportunity to take centre stage arrived, as they took on Tunisia at the Volgograd Arena. The Three Lions were fastest out of the blocks in that match and a raking pass from Jordan Henderson set Kane's club mate Dele Alli through into the Tunisian penalty area. Alli's cross was cleared before it could reach Raheem Sterling while Jesse Lingard got a shot in seconds later to force a fine save from Mouez Hassen.

England continued on the front foot and an exchange between Kane and Sterling saw the Spurs striker force a corner. Ashley Young delivered the kick, which was met by a John Stones header. Hassen saved again but the ball fell to Harry, who made no mistake from close range to put the Three Lions ahead. England managed 18 goal attempts during the match to Tunisia's five. Against the run of play though – and with their only effort on target – the Tunisians levelled ten minutes before half-time. Kane's former Spurs teammate Kyle Walker was penalised for an elbow on Fakhreddine Ben Youssef and Ferjani Sassi equalised from the spot.

Despite creating numerous goal-scoring opportunities in the second-half and boasting 60% possession, the match looked like ending in a frustrating 1-1 draw. To add insult to injury, there were two incidents when both the referee and Video Assistant Referee (VAR) failed to spot the England number nine being wrestled to the ground inside the Tunisian penalty area.

The 'jostling' continued as Kieran Trippier delivered a corner in stoppage time at the end of the game. Kane escaped the attentions of his markers and made a move to the back post. He was in the perfect position to get to a Harry Maguire flick-on to head past Tunisia's substitute goalkeeper Farouk Ben Mustapha. Cue scenes of wild celebration and relief all-round for the Three Lions.

Twenty two-year-old Charlie Brown was at four of England's World Cup matches in Russia and has fond memories of Kane's match winner.

"As that game (against Tunisia) went on, the expectation of a winner dwindled," said Brown. "As the time was running out, we needed that one man to step up and rise above others. I remember Kieran 'Whippier' (Trippier) as he will be now known, sending in a cross. I was tip-toed with an arm around my dad in expectation at the time. Maguire got up but didn't get enough on the ball to send it goal-wards. But instead it fell to the captain, Kane. As the coolest head in the stadium guided the ball home the pints went up and English fans erupted and our first victory (at the tournament) was completed!"

Belgium's 5-2 thrashing of Tunisia left England knowing a victory over Panama in their second group stage game in Nizhny Novgorod would guarantee them a place in the knockout phase. The only change to Southgate's starting line-up from the Three Lions' own win over the Tunisians came in midfield as Ruben Loftus-Cheek replaced the injured Dele Alli.

As per England's 2-1 victory over Tunisia, Southgate's side started well against Panama and took an eighth minute lead through a John Stones header. In the first-ever meeting between the two nations, Kane doubled the Three Lions' advantage, converting from the spot after Jesse Lingard had been fouled. Lingard got a goal of his own on 36 minutes, with a sweetly struck shot from the edge of the area while Stones got his second of the afternoon four minutes later. Another Kane penalty, after he was brought down by Fidel Escobar, gave England their first-ever, five-goal half-time lead at a major tournament.

17 minutes into the second half, Kane became the first England player to score a hat-trick at the World Cup since Gary Lineker in 1986 as Ruben Loftus-Cheek's shot from outside the area deflected off his ankle and flew past goalkeeper Jaime Penedo. Panama scored their first-ever World Cup goal with 12 minutes remaining as Felipe Baloy met a Ricardo Ávila free-kick with a sliding half-volley. The Central America nation celebrated but the afternoon of June 18 belonged to England and to Kane.

"It's rare England or any international team score so many goals," said Mark Heelis, who has attended nearly 100 England matches home and away since 2006, including the 6-1 win in Nizhny Novgorod. "I was at the England v Algeria game in Cape Town in 2010 where we were expected to win comfortably but it ended a disappointing 0-0 draw. So, to see England dominate the game from start to finish and be 5-0 up at half time… well, we were in dreamland.

"Panama came with a tactic to torment and frustrate, mainly by grappling and making it difficult for our players to find space from set pieces. This resulted in two penalties which Kane duly dispatched and the referee could easily have awarded more. The pick of the goals was Jesse Lingard's stunning strike from outside the box curling into the goalkeeper's top left corner. Kane's fortuitous third sent him on his way towards the Golden Boot with five goals in two games, with the 6-1 score line not flattering us in any way, shape or form.

"It was during this game the Gareth Southgate song (to the tune of Atomic Kitten's *Whole Again*) was born, demonstrating the new connection between the fans and the team. Southgate had worked hard on how the players interacted and engaged with fans and two wins from two had resulted in a new-found optimism. England were exciting to watch again. It felt like we were banishing demons from France 2016 in just two games, and boy it felt good. We stayed behind to belt out England songs to an empty stadium and any steward who would listen."

With his goal-scoring display against Panama, Kane equalled a number of records as he played his part in the Three Lions' biggest win at a major tournament. He became the first player to score at least twice in both of his first two World Cup appearances since Grzegorz Lato of Poland managed the same feat back in 1974. He matched Gary Lineker's goal scoring tally after two matches of the 1986 World Cup, when the *Match of the Day* presenter followed up a hat-trick against Poland with a brace against Paraguay. Kane also joined Lineker as just the third England player to score a hat-trick at the World Cup – the other being Sir Geoff Hurst, who managed a trio of goals in the 4-2 victory over West Germany in the final of 1966.

Matt Stewart, who was at every England game, up to and including the Three Lions' eventual semi-final appearance was impressed with Kane's start in Russia.

"I thought he was excellent in the two group games where he seemed energised and a real handful to the opposition," said Stewart. "His goal at the end of the Tunisia game was a poacher's goal and a sign of a player on form. His hat-trick against Panama might have included two penalties but these were won because of his forceful forward play."

As England confirmed their place in the knockout phase of the competition with one group game left to play, unsurprisingly, the odds of Kane becoming the tournament Golden Boot tumbled. After his hat-trick against Panama, the bookmakers installed him as 6/4 favourite.

Those who had wagered a bet on England's number nine topping the scoring charts would have been disappointed to learn of Gareth Southgate's decision to leave him on the bench for the match against Belgium, as the manager made a total of eight team changes for the Kaliningrad encounter on June 28. Opposite number Roberto Martinez made nine alterations for the game that would decide the winners of Group G.

It was Belgium who took the spoils in the fixture dubbed the 'battle of the reserves', scoring the only goal of the game six minutes into the second half. Former Manchester United winger Adnan Januzaj hit a well-placed shot into the top corner of Jordan Pickford's goal. Prior to kick-off, many commented that the route ahead for the winners of Group G might be tougher than for the runners-up. The team that topped the group was likely to meet Brazil if they got to the quarter-finals.

"It (England-Belgium) was a game where I didn't know what I wanted... the winning momentum or the better side of the draw," commented Brown, who was one of the thousands of England fans in Kaliningrad.

In the run-up to the match and asked to comment on whether he would prefer his team to finish first or second in the group, Southgate insisted England would "play to win" against Belgium. His decision to leave Kane on the bench for the entirety of the game – even after the Three Lions had gone behind – perhaps confirmed he was also not overly concerned at the prospect of defeat either.

Colombia's 1-0 victory earlier in the day saw them top Group H, meaning they would be England's opponents in the round of 16 on the back of the Three Lions ending up as Group G runners-up. The match with the South Americans – the 56th game of the tournament – was scheduled for the Spartak Stadium in Moscow on July 3 where the stage was set for captain Kane to return to Southgate's starting eleven.

CHAPTER TWO

FOOTBALL'S COMING HOME

The mood in Repino – as it had seemed throughout England's time in Russia – was relaxed in the days leading up to the round of 16 meeting with Colombia – the Three Lions' first knockout fixture at a World Cup in eight years.

Harry Kane gave his Twitter followers an insight into the vibe in the camp, posting a photograph of himself with Dele Alli and Kyle Walker on the back of the trio winning a 10k exercise bike challenge dubbed the 'Tour de Russia' by Ashley Young. It was another delightful image from the tournament that had also shown England players on the back of inflatable unicorns and throwing rubber chickens around their training pitch.

Final preparations for Colombia took place on the morning of July 2 ahead of the squad flying to Moscow for the match the following day. A confident-sounding Kane Tweeted, "Bring on tomorrow" with the now familiar Three Lions emoji and hashtags #ThreeLions #ENG #WorldCup. Speaking to the media ahead of the game, the skipper described the round of 16 clash as England's "moment of truth".

"Colombia are a tough team and have got some great players and we have to be ready for that," said Kane. "We have had a great start. This is the business end. It's a totally new tournament now. You focus on finding a way to win. There's going to be a bit more pressure on us now but I think it's important for us to have that mentality just to be calm in those situations, enjoy it still. This is what we train for and work hard for, these big moments, and hopefully we can do well. My confidence is sky high. That's 100 per cent the case. I think I am going to score every time I am on the pitch."

As the England coach arrived at the Spartak Stadium on July 3, it was clear that support for Colombia far outweighed England's following in Moscow. Just 1,520 England fans had purchased tickets for the match through the Football Association, while another 735 were sold through the FIFA allocation. Rough estimates were that England had around 7,000 supporters in the ground overall while it seemed Colombia at least doubled those numbers.

Kane was pitted against his club colleague Davinson Sanchez – the Calato-born centre-half who had an excellent debut season with Spurs in 2017-18. Quizzed about his upcoming duel with the England captain, Sanchez revealed that the 12 Tottenham players on international duty at the tournament had been keeping in touch via a WhatsApp group.

"Harry is a companero, a mate," Sanchez said. "I haven't spoken with him, although we've got a WhatsApp group there (at Tottenham) and we say congratulations to each other when we score or when we win. I'm happy for Harry because he's in a great moment but if I play against him, I'll try to stop him. Who we faced was not in my hands and I've also got Belgian teammates at Tottenham. But obviously being more familiar with the Premier League, I'm going to prefer England as opposition. Can we beat them? Anything is possible."

It was two Tottenham players who combined to provide the first half-chance of the match when Kieran Trippier's cross was met with a Kane header that went over the bar on 16 minutes. While the Three Lions looked to attack at every opportunity, Colombia seemed content to stifle their opponents. The tone for what resulted in an ill-tempered contest – there were 36 fouls and eight yellow cards – was set shortly before half-time when Wilmar Barrios seemed lucky to escape a red card for an apparent headbutt on Jordan Henderson.

"I felt England were comfortable aside from the unpleasant tactics from Colombia, who seemed hell bent on ruining the game as a spectacle," commented England fan Matt Stewart, watching that evening in the Spartak Stadium.

Colombia's 'unpleasant tactics' continued in the second period and they were duly punished when referee Mark Geiger awarded

England a penalty after Kane was hauled down by Carlos Sanchez. 'Los Cafeteros' players confronted Geiger, delaying the taking of Kane's spot-kick. During the melee, Jefferson Lerma could be seen scuffing the penalty spot while Jordan Henderson was booked. The whole period of time between the penalty being awarded and the kick being thrashed into the back of David Ospina's net was a staggering three minutes and 26 seconds.

Author Duncan Alexander (@oilysailor) offered a comical take on the episode, Tweeting:

"If you start (the New Order song) *World In Motion* when England win their penalty vs Colombia, John Barnes' rap has just finished when Kane eventually scores."

Ed Malyon from *The Independent* described the England captain as the "King of Calm" for stepping up to convert the penalty and added: "He (Kane) had the cool head to score when his team needed it most." The skipper's successful penalty conversation saw him become the first England player to score in six consecutive international appearances since Tommy Lawton back in 1939.

"Holding the ball, wandering around and gathering his thoughts, Kane was in the middle of a storm," Malyon described. "From when England's penalty was awarded in the 54th minute after he had been wrestled to the ground it was almost exactly three more that the ball was in Kane's arms, and around him were yellow shirts screaming and remonstrating, red shirts pushing and pulling while a black shirt struggled.

"As referee Mark Geiger flailed in a hornet's nest of professional footballers, desperately trying to work out who had stung who, Kane breathed deeply. Even after those three minutes had passed, there were twenty-six more seconds with the ball on the ground, sat on the penalty spot that had been deliberately scuffed by Colombia's Jefferson Lerma. But then there was calm. David Ospina waited as long as he could but eventually had to bite, diving low and right. Kane slightly adjusted his strike to clip the ball home around waist-height and as it rippled the net, the calmness exploded into celebration."

As the match continued, Kane seemed to be a particular target for Los Cafeteros' rough approach to the tie. The Tottenham striker was on the end of nine fouls – the greatest number of offences committed on an England player in a World Cup match since Tunisia fouled Alan Shearer eleven times in 1998.

As the match entered its final minute, Mateus Uribe's long-range effort forced a world-class save from Jordan Pickford who dived to his left to keep out a shot bound for the top corner. Such a moment of quality from the Everton goalkeeper seemed deserving of victory. But before supporters had the opportunity to see a replay of Pickford's heroics on the stadium's big screens, Yerry Mina scored with a downward header from a Juan Cuadrado corner to send the game into extra-time. Mina's goal – after 92 minutes and 33 seconds – was the first time England had conceded in stoppage time at the end of a World Cup match.

Substitute Danny Rose came the closest to scoring for either side in the added period, with his cross-come-shot flashing agonisingly across the Colombian six-yard box and missing Ospina's far post by a whisker. The final whistle signalled England's fourth penalty shootout at a World Cup – the previous three had yielded defeats to West Germany in 1990, Argentina in 1998 and Portugal in 2006.

Radamel Falcao scored for Colombia with their opening kick of the shootout, while Kane was assured with his effort to equalise, blasting the ball to Ospina's right. Juan Cuadrado, Marcus Rashford and Luis Muriel continued the 100% conversion rate as Los Cafeteros led 3-2. What followed was a moment of seeming heartbreak for England as a penalty from Jordan Henderson was stopped by an excellent save from Ospina.

The Three Lions were handed a lifeline when Mateus Uribe's effort from 12 yards cannoned back off the woodwork.

Kieran Trippier's shot levelled the scores and then Jordan Pickford produced an incredible one-handed stop from Carlos Bacca to make it advantage England. Eric Dier promptly stepped up to score and secure a 4-3 victory, ending the Three Lions' story of penalty woes at the World Cup. It was their first shoot-out win at a major tournament since beating Spain at Wembley in the quarter-final of UEFA Euro 1996.

Amidst the euphoria following the penalty shoot-out success, there was a feeling amongst England fans out in Russia and back in blighty that maybe, just maybe, football was 'coming home'.

Kane's role in the victory over Colombia was widely praised with the BBC's Chief Football Writer Phil McNulty giving him a nine out of ten rating for his display. "England's leader. Showed great nerve for his penalties and takes on all the responsibility with supreme character," he wrote. There was praise closer to home for Kane too. His fiancée Kate Goodland commented on Instagram: "Still buzzing, so so so so so proud of you @harrykane #neverindoubt #footballscominghome."

There was a war of words after the match. England defender John Stones described Colombia as "probably the dirtiest team" he had ever played against while Colombia manager Jose Pekerman accused the Three Lions of feigning fouls. "(England) players fall in the box," he said. "They collide and fall. It's hurtful." With six of the eight yellow cards awarded that night going to Colombian players, Stones had perhaps greater evidence to support his claim.

Kane meanwhile said the penalty shootout victory over Colombia was a coming of age for a young England team;

"We spoke a lot about being an inexperienced, young team, but we grew up a lot on that pitch tonight. It was mixed emotions, highs and lows, even in the penalty shootouts. The boys were fantastic. It will give us huge belief. There's still a long way to go, but as a team we are as together as we can be. This will give the team more belief than ever, and the fans back home.

"(There were) so many emotions in that game. I thought we played well, controlled the game, and obviously we were so unlucky to concede last minute. Penalty shootouts are a lot about mentality, and obviously we know England haven't done great in the past, so it was nice to get that one off our back and it'll give us huge belief going forward."

Prior to the World Cup beginning, those supporters optimistic enough to plot England's possible route to the quarter-finals would have been expecting a meeting with Brazil or Germany. The so-called 'winners curse' – that has seen the last three world champions eliminated at the group stage of the following tournament – struck for the third successive occasion at Russia 2018 as Germany made an early exit. Brazil meanwhile were paired – and subsequently beaten – by Belgium in the last eight. So instead, it was Sweden – who overcame Switzerland in the round of 16 – who lay in wait for the Three Lions.

Kane, who reportedly experienced discomfort in his calf after the bruising victory over Colombia, was declared fit in advance of the quarter-final showdown with Sweden in Samara on July 7. In the pre-match press conference, he talked of the unity that existed within the England camp.

"We are just like family, really," Kane said. "We've spent a lot of time together. We all get on very well. I spoke about the togetherness and trust before the tournament, but we always want to prove it on the pitch. We have done that so far. It's made us even stronger.

"After that game (versus Colombia) the other night the joy in everyone's face, we had worked so hard to come through that, and it makes us even more proud of each other. I look at them as my brothers, and I know they look at me the same. We will do anything for each other and that is what we have to do for the rest of the tournament."

The closeness that Kane spoke of was picked up on by England supporters. "The main thing I take from the group is the togetherness of the squad," said Charlie Brown, who attended the Three Lions' group matches and semi-final in Russia. "Following England around Russia – not only physically but on social media – it was clear to see the chemistry." On July 8, *Three Lions* by Baddiel & Skinner and The Lightening Seeds topped the UK Singles Chart for the first time since 1998, reflecting the togetherness England fans at home felt with their team too. 'Football's Coming Home' was certainly an improvement on the efforts of former Voice judge Ricky Wilson and cricket legend Freddie Flintoff. They released an unofficial anthem for Kane during the tournament to the tune of Boney M's 1978 hit *Rasputin*, containing cringeworthy lyrics such as "Ra Ra Rasputin, England's got a goal machine, he's Harry Kane and he's gonna score."

With support for Kane and his England teammates growing by the day, Danny Greaves – son of Tottenham legend and World Cup winner Jimmy Greaves – revealed a message of support his father had given Harry before the tournament;

Speaking to the *Daily Mirror*, Danny said: "My dad told Harry to go and break all of his records and win the World Cup too. The dream would be for England to win it and for Harry to go one better than my dad by scoring the winner in the final."

Sir Geoff Hurst, who replaced the injured Greaves in the 1966 World Cup Final and subsequently scored a hat-trick in the 4-2 victory against West Germany, added his words of encouragement: "You will never have a better opportunity to make the country proud," he said.

There was a touching moment ahead of the quarter-final when Kane learnt the story of five-year-old cancer patient Ben Williams. Staff at Queen Elizabeth Hospital in Birmingham had filmed a video of football-fanatic Ben receiving a replica of the World Cup trophy after undergoing an intensive six-week period of radiotherapy. Ben's radiographer Liam Herbert tweeted the footage to the England captain and was amazed by Harry's reply, which read:

"Hi Ben, I've seen your video and you are an inspiration. Carry on fighting and we'll do everything we can on Saturday to keep a smile on your face! #BensWorldCup"

Following Kane's response, Ben's parents spoke to ITV News about the exchange. "When we saw the message from Harry Kane – that's what this has been all about, to get Ben's favourite player to give him a shout out," said father Sam Williams. "It's been a fantastic couple of days. We couldn't be any more happy with the guys at the hospital for arranging this for us, for arranging the ceremony yesterday and for getting Ben through what's been an incredibly tough six weeks."

During the World Cup, Data Powa revealed that Harry was the fourth-most searched for player online after Neymar, Lionel Messi and Cristiano Ronaldo. From the start of the tournament to the end of the quarter-final stage, a staggering 96,825,600 searches for the England skipper's name had been conducted across all social media platforms and search engines worldwide. There was no need for Sweden skipper Andreas Granqvist to Google Kane's name though, as he was already well aware of the threat the England captain posed to his side.

"We know they have Harry Kane, who is really dangerous in the penalty box, so we need to be very strong in the box and try to make sure that they don't get the service that they need," Granqvist said. "He's good at everything and it's going to be a very tough match against him. But we're going to do everything to stop him."

Compared with the hard-fought match against Colombia in the previous round, the quarter-final with Sweden felt far more comfortable for Gareth Southgate's men. "It was a controlled performance overall and, importantly, the four players who would have missed the semi-final had they received another booking remained out of the referee's notebook," summarised Daniel Taylor on England's display in his match report for *The Observer*.

In the 24th meeting between the two nations, Kane had a decent opportunity to open the scoring on 19 minutes but dragged his shot wide. Harry Maguire headed England in front on the half hour mark from an out-swinging Ashley Young corner. It was the fourth time the Three Lions had scored from a corner and their eighth goal in ten that had arrived from a set-piece situation at the tournament.

A feature of England's set-pieces at the World Cup was a corner routine dubbed the 'love train' by ITV co-commentator Glenn Hoddle during the match against Colombia. It was in evidence again prior to Maguire's goal against Sweden, as a collection of Three Lions players stood together in the centre of the penalty area before breaking off in different directions as the ball was delivered. The Leicester City defender rose above his marker Emil Forsberg and powered his header into the back of the net. Sweden's best chance to equalise came shortly after the interval when a Marcus Berg effort forced a save from Jordan Pickford before England extended their lead.

On 58 minutes, Jesse Lingard delivered a cross to the far post which was headed in by Dele Alli. The header, which was England's 11th goal at the tournament, saw the Three Lions equal their best-ever scoring tally at a World Cup set back in the glory days of 1966. Alli became the country's second youngest player to score at the competition at 22 years and 87 days after Michael Owen, who netted against Romania in 1998 aged just 18 years and 190 days.

With less than 20 minutes remaining, Pickford tipped another effort from Berg over the crossbar as the goalkeeper kept his first clean sheet of the tournament, making three saves in total during the match. The 2-0 victory over Sweden confirmed the Three Lions' first World Cup semi-final appearance since 1990 and their first match in the last four of a major competition since Euro '96.

"Typically watching England at 1-0 can be uncomfortable," commented England fan Mark Heelis, who was inside the Samara Arena that afternoon. "We saw it against Colombia – a team getting deeper and deeper and inviting pressure on. Not this time though. We looked confident and positive against Sweden, looking for a second. It was a strange feeling – for once I felt we wouldn't lose and when Alli headed in a second we all knew we were about to qualify for only our second World Cup semi-final outside England. And the fans duly responded in the stands – it was a party atmosphere – grown men hugging each other and dancing in the aisles. We weren't going home this time."

Kane reflected with pride on England's performance against Sweden as he and his team mates awaited the result of the Russia-Croatia tie in Sochi to discover their semi-final opponents.

"It was a difficult game, Sweden made it tough – long balls, different to what we have faced so far," Kane said after the match. "But we were brilliant at set-pieces, crosses into the box and we are buzzing. We know there is a big game ahead with the semi-final but we are feeling good and we're confident. We just have to go again. We are enjoying it and we've got to keep doing what we are doing and make the country proud."

In *The Observer's* player ratings section, Martha Kelner gave Kane seven out of ten for his display and commented: "A rare game off the scoresheet for the leading Golden Boot candidate but still played an essential role in bullying the Sweden defence." Phil McNulty agreed with Kelner's assessment on the BBC Sport website, giving the Spurs striker a six, adding; "One of his quieter days but always available and worked so hard."

England's players celebrated their victory over Sweden by climbing into the stands of the Samara Arena to meet up with friends and family, while Kane and his teammates also signed autographs for travelling fans. Back in the UK, an audience of 19.9million tuned in to watch the match – with that figure not including an estimated 3.5million who headed to pubs across the country and a further 3.5million on BBC iPlayer. The nation, basking in day upon day of glorious sunshine at that time, was gripped by World Cup fever.

CHAPTER THREE

END OF A DREAM

Croatia's penalty shootout victory over hosts Russia set-up a semi-final meeting with England – the Three Lions' first appearance at that stage of the competition for 28 years. For many, the progress of Gareth Southgate's men to the last four had exceeded expectations. Not Harry Kane's though – he said England could win the World Cup before a ball was even kicked and insisted his team wouldn't be satisfied unless they reached the final.

"We are one step closer to what is the biggest game in football as a professional," said the captain in in the lead-up to the Luzhniki Stadium semi-final. "We said we wanted to write our own history. Hopefully we can go one step further than 1990 and get to the final. It's been a long time since England have done well in a major tournament, and we've got a tough game coming up against Croatia, but we feel confident.

"We felt so composed against Sweden and, looking around, everyone was on the same wavelength. Everyone was calm and that's what we need if we want to go all the way. We had that sense before the game that we didn't want to go home just yet. We don't want to let anyone down and we want to be here until the end. Now we're one step closer. We are not finished yet. Everyone wants to finish the job and go all the way."

The Croatia semi-final set-up an interesting personal battle for Kane against the Liverpool defender Dejan Lovren. When the pair met in Tottenham's 4-1 victory at Wembley earlier in the season, Harry's dominance was such that Reds manager Jurgen Klopp substituted the centre-half after just 31 minutes. Later in the season – as Kane was retrospectively awarded with a goal against Stoke originally credited to Christian Eriksen – Lovren took a sly dig at the Spurs striker. In an Instagram conversation with Mohamed Salah – vying with Kane for both the Premier League Golden Boot and PFA Player of the Year crown – the Croatian mentioned 'Mr Touch' in their chat – a clear reference to Harry.

Kane never responded to Lovren's childish quip but months later, as Croatia prepared to take on England, journalists were keen to bring up the topic of the pair's past meeting at Wembley.

"I don't know what to say in response to this question," snapped Lovren. "It's completely irrelevant, that 4-1 defeat against Tottenham. Why didn't you ask me how I played well against him? You are just nit-picking my poor performances.

"I have all respect for Harry Kane. He has been showing season in, season out, that he's one of the best strikers in the Premier League. He is constant. He bangs in goals. He's one of the greatest threats but he's not alone. His team mates play at top-drawer clubs. It's going to be a difficult task for all of us. But if we are ready to give our all on (the) pitch like we did when we played Argentina, if we will be compact, then I don't believe that there will be problems."

In the run-up to the semi-final showdown, Croatian tabloid *24 Hours*, attempted to dismiss the threat Kane posed Lovren and co – based on two matches they had seen him play four years ago. Recalling his performances in Under-21 meetings with Croatia in 2014, writer Dejan Lovric branded the striker as a "poor reincarnation of Peter Crouch" and "slower than a snail".

"He puts the ball on his chest, loses the duel and falls to the turf," added Lovric. "The ball ran away from him as if he were shovelling it. He decides to dribble but falls."

Former Spurs captain Michael Dawson was far better placed to provide a measured assessment of Kane's four-year journey since establishing himself in the Spurs first-team to captaining England at a World Cup. In an interview with Tottenham Hotspur's official website, Dawson said: "Harry's just continued doing what he's done for a few years now, and that's scoring goals on the big stage.

He's captain of England and the way he carries himself, he's a credit to Spurs and England.

"You don't get to where he's got to without hard work. He got his opportunity four years ago and he hasn't looked back. He's really taken off. He stays out of the limelight and the only way he gets into the media is through what he does on the pitch. He was so focused in those earlier days, so driven to be successful. The rewards he's getting now haven't come without that graft."

The Guardian's Daniel Taylor described the mood back in England as "delirium" prior to the semi-final. Fans woke up on the morning of July 11 to #WaistcoatWednesday trending on Twitter, as photos of those paying their sartorial tributes to Gareth Southgate emerged. A Harry Kane lookalike called Danny McLaughlin was a guest on ITV's *Lorraine* show while artist Graham Short told BBC Hereford and Worcester of his efforts to etch mini portraits of the England captain on 11 £5 notes – to be released if the Three Lions reached the final. Short's previous micro-engravings of Jane Austen on £5 notes were valued at £50,000 each when they were circulated in 2016. The 11 Kane fivers were eventually destroyed, but six different notes – each with a portrait marking one of Harry's six World Cup goals – made their way into circulation instead.

That wasn't the only artistic tribute to Kane as a striking graffiti work by Gustavo Nenao emerged in Leake Street tunnel (www. leakestreetarches.london) in London, close to Waterloo Station. Featuring a graphic of Harry celebrating a goal at the tournament, with supporters cheering in the background, it also included the words 'It's Coming Home'. A slightly more obscure homage to the striker came as artist Nathan Wyburn used gravy to 'paint' an image of the England skipper across 40 Pukka Pies. The company behind the publicity stunt offered free pies to up to 50 people called Harry Kane.

Despite being outnumbered by their Croatian counterparts, an estimated 10,000 England fans helped create a carnival-like feel at the Luzhniki Stadium. Thousands of extra supporters travelled to the game after a tranche of tickets were released on the FIFA website four days before the semi-final. "The pre-match atmosphere was incredible especially as there had been an influx of extra fans," said Matt Stewart, who was at his sixth match of the tournament. "The English were in fine vocal form with the stadium filling quickly," added Charlie Brown.

Kane looked calm and composed as he led his teammates out into the cauldron of noise for England's most important match since the semi-final with Germany at UEFA Euro '96. Just four minutes into the game, Dele Alli was felled by Luka Modric in close proximity to the Croatian penalty area. Kieran Trippier – one of the undoubted star turns of the World Cup for England – stepped up to take the resulting free-kick and guided it into the top corner of Danijel Subasic's goal.

"As soon as it left his (Trippier's) foot I was up and boy did the stadium rock," reflected Brown on England's opening goal. Lawrence Ostlere of *The Independent* went on to describe Trippier's freekick as: "…representing one of England's greatest triumphs in Russia: that ability to make unbridled joy ripple out."

"In that split second when it all happened, when the Croatian wall turned to see, when Danijel Subasic came back to earth empty handed, when the net bulged and Kieran Trippier tore across the Luzhniki, a version of the same few words flitted through English minds, while wide-eyed and incredulous: it really is coming home. If England's World Cup can be broken down into a rollercoaster of belief and doubt, of hope and despair, then that moment was its terrifying peak, when the wall of inhibitions melted away and the possibilities seemed endless," wrote Ostlere.

In a commanding first-half performance, chances arrived for the Three Lions to increase their lead. A fine through-ball from Jesse Lingard presented Kane with an opportunity on the half-hour mark. England's number nine forced a decent save from Subasic and with the follow up, crashed his effort against the post with the goalkeeper appearing to get the slightest touch. The linesman raised his flag after the ball went out of play to signal offside, but replays showed the England captain was on.

Croatia – and particularly their playmakers Luka Modric, Ivan Perisic and Ivan Rakitic – began to exert their influence on the game in the second-half. Rakitic found Sime Vrsaljko with a neat pass 23 minutes into the second period and the right-back's subsequent cross was flicked in by Perisic for the equaliser. Four minutes later, he struck the ball beyond the dive of England goalkeeper Jordan Pickford but his effort came back off the far post to the Three Lions' relief.

By the time Turkish referee Cuneyt Cakir blew the final whistle to signal extra-time, England looked jaded and Croatia well in command. However, Southgate's men seemed to draw on extra reserves in the added period. Stones' header from a corner nine minutes in almost re-established their lead but for a magnificent goal-line clearance from Vrsaljko. The threat at the other end was demonstrated by Mario Mandzukic, who forced a brave save from Pickford.

The killer blow to England's hopes of a first World Cup Final appearance since 1966 came four minutes into the second period as Mandzukic got on the end of a Perisic header and fired past Pickford. Try as they might, the Three Lions were unable to forge any clear-cut chances after that and bowed out of the tournament.

"The game hinged on two good chances (in the first half of normal time) that England failed to take – one by Kane, the other by Lingard," lamented England fan Matt Stewart. "Eventually we succumbed to a technically superior side with a lot more experience. The disappointment was palpable... will we ever get this chance again?"

Kane drew his own conclusions, as he spoke to ITV after the match: "'It is tough, we are gutted, we worked so hard and the fans were amazing. It was a tough game, a 50-50 game, I'm sure we will look back and there is stuff we could've done better.

"It hurts, it hurts a lot, but we can hold our heads up high – we have gone further than a lot of people thought we would do. We created some good chances being 1-0 up, there are lots of ifs and buts and it is hard in these games, it is small margins and it went their way today. Until they scored we were always under the cosh. There is a lot we could have done better but they played better."

The following day, the England skipper took to Twitter to offer further thoughts and send an extended message to supporters;

"A lot of emotions today," he wrote. "First of all I'm so proud of this team and staff for giving everything we could over a long period of time together. We have overcome so many challenges that have haunted England in the past. We have reconnected with our amazing supporters and have enjoyed this incredible experience together. It wasn't the outcome we wanted and as painful as it is right now, I'm sure we will learn an awful lot from last night's game. It's time now to hold our heads high as a nation and be proud of each other. I'm excited to be part of this team and the challenge to improve going forward. Thank you all for your support! #WorldCup #ENG #ThreeLions"

In the UK, a peak audience of 26.5 million people watched England's semi-final against Croatia – the highest British TV viewing figures since the 2012 Olympic opening ceremony and the fourth-highest figure overall of the last 25 years. The Duke of Cambridge, president of the Football Association, tweeted his reaction to the Three Lions' performances in Russia:

"I know how disappointed @england must feel right now but I couldn't be more proud of this team and you should hold your heads high," he wrote. "You've had an incredible #WorldCup, made history, and gave us fans something to believe in. We know there is more to come from this @england team. W"

Liverpool striker Daniel Sturridge, who had played for England at their two previous major tournaments added:

"If anyone has anything negative to say about this @England team or individuals keep your tweets to yourself. Nobody would have thoughts (sic) they'd be where they are or achieved what they have and they've made everyone proud so get behind them and show love not hate #threelions ♥"

During the tournament, London-based journalist Ceylan Yeginsu wrote an article for *The New York Times* under the headline 'World Cup Brings England Together at a Time of Division'. "Much of the nation seems determined to take a timeout from the acrimonious politics and bask in something recently in short supply: Unity, not to mention blind hope," was Yeginsu's take on the positive impact the Three Lions' performances brought to a nation.

For all the good that England's national football team brought the country in the summer of 2018 there was still a minority that felt the need to pour scorn on Gareth Southgate's squad. Just minutes after the final whistle sounded in Moscow, talkSPORT posted an article on their website which compiled a host of critical Twitter comments aimed at Harry Kane. "Kane is a fraud," wrote one 'fan', "Kane hasn't been involved at all has he?" said another.

In an article entitled, 'Don't listen to the keyboard warriors, Harry Kane is a deserving Golden Boot winner', *i* journalist Oliver Young-Myles addressed the madness of those who felt inclined to run down the England captain despite topping the scoring charts in Russia.

"Kane finished two goals clear of any other player at the World Cup in Russia and captained the team to a semi-final, England's best finish since 1990," wrote Young-Myles. "Given such achievements, Kane has been lauded as a national treasure since touching back down in England, right? Well, not quite.

"Instead there seems to be a growing sentiment that Kane actually endured a pretty poor tournament despite his six goals. He has been accused of 'stat-padding': a phrase which seems to have derived solely from Twitter and insinuates that strikers like Kane are flat-track bullies, scoring the majority of their goals against sub-standard opposition.

"Tunisia, who were ranked the highest of the five African nations competing in this World Cup and a Panama team that qualified at the USA's expense, have since been dismissed as little more than pub teams. It would be interesting to see whether the same fans would dismiss Antoine Griezmann's goal scoring contribution to France's World Cup win given three of his four goals were penalties."

During the World Cup, Kane spoke of the negative effect reading social media had on him when he was at the European Championships two years earlier. "For me, it's to stay away from the hype of it all," said Kane, when asked what the biggest lesson he had learnt from UEFA Euro 2016 was. "I was so excited about the Euros, being on Twitter all the time or being on news apps. You want to see what everyone is talking about. This tournament (Russia 2018) I've changed that and stayed off social media as much as possible."

England's memorable World Cup in Russia ended with a fixture described by Alan Shearer as "utter stupidity... the last thing any player wants" and the match that "should never be played" by Louis van Gaal. The pair were of course referring to the tournament's third place play-off. While the occasion is one many players, managers and even some fans could do without, Kane was relishing the opportunity of taking on Belgium in Saint Petersburg on July 14. After all, it gave him the chance to extend his lead at the top of the Golden Boot list, which stood at six goals prior to the game – two more than his nearest challengers, which included the Red Devils' Romelu Lukaku.

Belgium took an early lead in the game, played in front of a crowd of 64,406. Thomas Meunier won the race with England defender Danny Rose to get to Nacer Chadli's cross and fired them ahead inside four minutes. The Three Lions responded and when Raheem Sterling teed-up Kane with a clear shot on goal on 23 minutes, it seemed like the net was about to bulge. Instead, the striker miscued and his right-foot effort went harmlessly wide.

No less than six Tottenham players started the match with Kane joined in the Three Lions' line-up by Eric Dier, Kieran Trippier and Rose while Toby Alderweireld and Jan Vertonghen were part of Belgium's backline. The Spurs quota rose in the second period when Mousa Dembele came on as a substitute for Youri Tielemans and Dele Alli replaced Ruben Loftus-Cheek. Before the half-time whistle sounded, Alderweireld nearly doubled Belgium's lead with a well struck volley from a corner that went just over Jordan Pickford's bar.

Another Spurs man, Dier, played a one-two with substitute Marcus Rashford midway through the second-half. Faced with the on-rushing Thibaut Courtois, Dier dinked the ball over the Chelsea stopper only for Alderweireld to clear his effort off the line. The best football of the game came ten minutes from time as the Belgians launched a swift, passing move that ended in a Meunier volley forcing a fine save from Pickford. The Red Devils managed just four shots on goal during the game to England's six but they made their chances count, with Eden Hazard sealing a 2-0 win for his side on 82 minutes.

"This game showed there is still room for improvement," Kane told ITV after the defeat. "We're not the finished article, we're still improving and will only get better. We don't want to wait another 20 years to get into the semi-finals and the big matches. We need to improve, we need to get better but that will come. We have made huge strides. Now it is about resting up and getting ready for the next season.

"The lads couldn't have given any more. Belgium are obviously a good team. I can't fault the lads, we gave everything. We wanted to finish on a high. We're disappointed not to have won the game but it shows we can still learn and hold our head up high."

Just before the final whistle sounded in Saint Petersburg, ITV commentator Sam Matterface asked co-commentator Glenn Hoddle about his thoughts on Harry's tournament;

"When he looks back at his tournament, (will he think) first-half good, second-half could have been better?" quizzed Matterface. "Without doubt," replied Hoddle. "It's not the Harry that we've seen (earlier in the tournament). The first-half against Colombia, I thought was his best (performance). He held it (the ball) up, he had movement. Since then, I don't know if he's got a knock or something. His movement has been restricted. It looks like he's going to come out (of the tournament) as the top goal scorer."

Statistics back-up Hoddle's suggestion that Harry's World Cup was something of a tale of two halves. He ended the tournament with six goals from six shots on target but had just one shot on target in his final four games – his penalty against Colombia in the last 16. Facts and figures can only ever tell part of a story though and at times during the competition, the supply to Kane from his teammates was limited. While Croatia for example boast playmakers such as Luka Modric, Ivan Perisic and Ivan Rakitic, it's widely acknowledged that England lack a genuine 'trequartista' of their own.

What shouldn't be overlooked is the major role Kane and England played in what was a magnificent World Cup in Russia

– one which produced 169 goals in 64 matches. The final of the tournament was in keeping with the previous 31 days of football we had seen, as France beat Croatia 4-2 at the Luzhniki Stadium on July 15. It was a Spurs player who got his hands on the World Cup after the game –≠ French skipper Hugo Lloris lifted the most famous trophy of them all amidst a heavy downpour in Moscow.

The trophy presentation included the announcement of the various personal awards for the competition. Belgium goalkeeper Courtois was named as the winner of the Golden Gloves, French sensation Kylian Mbappe took the young player award and Croatia's Modric was crowned as the player of the tournament, collecting the Golden Ball. Having notched five group-stage goals and then a penalty in the round of 16 victory over Colombia, Harry Kane became the first Englishman to win the Golden Boot since Gary Lineker in 1986. For reasons unknown, Kane's name was jeered by sections of the Moscow crowd – fellow non-attendee Courtois, received no such negative response neither did Mbappe or Modric. The incident served to illustrate that while he has many millions of fans, the Tottenham striker has now reached such a pinnacle in his career that he is also a target for the haters.

England's World Cup heroes returned to the UK on July 15. The last time the Three Lions had reached the semi-final of the competition in 1990, around 300,000 people lined the streets of Luton for an open-top bus parade – best remembered for Paul Gascoigne wearing a pair of fake breasts. There were no such scenes when the class of 2018 touched down at Birmingham Airport. At the request of the Football Association, fans were asked to stay away from the airport – with its lack of a suitable public viewing area. "It's not my decision but I agree with the decision," said Southgate, on the announcement there would not be a parade this time. "If we'd made the final it's maybe different."

Around 400 fans still turned up at Birmingham Airport and managed to find a vantage point to cheer England's charter jet as it landed at 3:50pm – ten minutes before the World Cup Final kicked-off. Live footage of the low-key 'event' was shown on the UK's news channels, as Kane and his teammates assembled for a photograph on the steps of the plane. Raheem Sterling was seen kicking a football on the tarmac before the players and staff said their goodbyes and got into a convoy of Mercedes-Benz cars.

Kane spent the next few days with his heavily pregnant fiancée Kate and the rest of his family before travelling to the 147th Open at Carnoustie. The striker revealed to journalists that he was planning to cut short his holiday by two weeks ahead of the start of the 2018-19 Premier League season. He also said that he was looking to break a particular career duck in the coming weeks – scoring a senior goal in the month of August for the first time.

"I will hopefully be back for the first game and hopefully try and score in August this year," he commented. "I want to be playing in four weeks' time. We'll have to talk to the gaffer at Spurs."

Reflecting on the World Cup, Kane added: "It's been a fantastic campaign, for me personally and the team. It's something I'm very proud of. But there's still stuff I can improve on. I can get better. I feel like there have been games in this tournament when I could have done better, but that's all part of the learning curve. It's a big achievement. Not many people get to say they've won a Golden Boot at a World Cup. I said coming into this tournament that I wanted to prove I could do it on these stages."

CHAPTER FOUR

THE EARLY DAYS

Some 25 years before his World Cup heroics in Russia, Harry Edward Kane was born in the same east London hospital (Whipps Cross) as his future hero, David Beckham, on July 28, 1993. Given his current allegiances for country and club, it seemed fitting that Harry was born under the astrological sign of Leo and in the Chinese Year of the Rooster. Appropriately too, for a boy who would one day go on to be heralded by Spurs fans as 'one of their own', he was raised just a few miles from White Hart Lane in Chingford – in the heart of Tottenham-supporting country – where he lived with mother Kim, father Pat and older brother Charlie.

Harry's dad Pat originally hails from Galway in the Republic of Ireland, with his paternal grandfather Michael – who passed away in 2013 – having originally brought the Kane family to England as a young man. Prior to the striker making his senior debut for England, Ireland manager Martin O'Neill says Kane once expressed an interest in playing for his father's homeland.

"The order of events, though I don't think it's really important any more, is that initially the agent (of Harry Kane) got in touch and said that he would have a keen interest, and we wanted to go and chase it up,' O'Neill told the *Daily Mail* in the weeks leading up to Kane's England debut against Lithuania in 2015. "But then I noticed in the newspaper where he said he wanted to play for England. And that has remained the same."

Harry – like so many millions of boys and girls – grew up loving football almost from the minute he could kick a ball. In an article he wrote for *The Players' Tribune* in 2018, he recalled his memories of his formative years, playing with dad Pat and brother Charlie.

"There was this park right behind our house in Chingford, and I'd go there all the time with my dad and my brother to play football. No goals. No proper pitch. Just give us some grass and we were happy."

While it was Pat and Charlie who were Harry's regular playing partners, Kane has suggested his footballing ability might be down to his mum Kim and specifically, her father and his late granddad Eric Hogg, who died from cancer around 15 years ago. Midfielder Eric played at a semi-professional level for the likes of Brentwood and Warley during the 1960s and family members say they see a similarity in the way both Eric and Harry move on a football pitch.

"I think the sporting genes come from my Mum's side of the family although the topic is a hot debate in the Kane household," Harry once said. "Dad probably won't like me saying that, but I think my grandad Eric on my Mum's side was quite a good footballer, and played at a decent level"

On June 30, 2018, the *Daily Mirror* ran a front-page story on Eric and Harry with its headline reading "Thanks Eric… for giving us Harry Kane!" accompanied with a sub-headline "Football-mad grandad inspired England captain". In the article itself, the newspaper interviewed Harry's great aunt Bette Bovington about her late-brother Eric.

"He (Eric) knew Harry would play for one of the big clubs, but he hoped it would end up being Arsenal," joked Bette – a life-long supporter of the Gunners – in the article.

Harry went to Larkswood Primary Academy before following in the footsteps of his hero Beckham by attending Chingford Foundation School between 2004 and 2009. "Beckham was a big inspiration to me growing up," Kane told the Football Association's official website. "Going to the same school as him showed what was possible for me in my career. I got to meet him when he launched his academy at the O2 Arena in 2005. I also got to meet him when he came to train at Spurs, which was great for me. Beckham was obviously a world-class player who has done a lot for this game and a lot for this country. He was a big role model for me and hopefully I can have a career as good as his."

Like 'Becks', as well as future Spurs team mate Andros Townsend, Harry played for local side Ridgeway Rovers. He attended one of the club's annual trials in the Autumn of 1999, with coach and current Tottenham Hotspur scout Dave Bricknell remembering the occasion well.

"This six-year-old boy (Kane) turns up at Loughton Rugby Club, and we're doing a little shooting session, and I ask for a lad who can go in goal," Bricknell told a special BBC Radio 5 Live documentary on Kane in 2016. "This little boy puts his hand up and says, 'I'll go in goal'. So, we give him some gloves, and he performs heroics – makes some fantastic saves. I think, yes, I've got a goalkeeper here – because goalkeepers are very hard to find, particularly at six. They do it for five seconds and they want to be a centre-forward.

"Then I get told he's not a goalkeeper. So, I think, OK, and I stick (him) on (the) pitch. And he's scoring loads of goals, on a very long pitch as well, so he ends up being our striker. He could see a pass, he could play. He was very, very good at an early age. He could strike a ball... He had a good touch, but his main attribute was that he had major confidence in himself."

Harry also played for his school teams, with his footballing ability obvious to those who coached him there.

"Harry was very technically talented and gifted right from the word go in Year Seven," Mark Leadon – the former Head of PE and now Assistant Headteacher at Chingford Foundation School – told the *Waltham Forest Guardian* back in 2015.

Harry's human qualities shone at the school as much as his footballing ability. "He was conscientious, behaved himself and was a good all-round sportsman," adds Leadon. "He was a good cricketer, but it was obvious he was a class footballer. He never saw himself as a superstar, he just got on with it.

"One of the things that stands out now at Tottenham is his work ethic. He was exactly the same here and always gave 100 per cent."

Denis McElligott – English teacher and Kane's former school football team manager – is also full of praise for him:

"Harry was clever, articulate and very humble. He was not flash at all and must have known he was brilliant but was always very generous with the other kids – never distant or aloof. He was a little bit stocky but then you would see him after a game just going out running, losing weight and working on his fitness. It was unbelievable.

"Kids from other schools started to know who he was and know his name. He was doing ridiculous things – scoring from corners and halfway lines. If we were struggling during a game, the tactic would be 'just give it to Harry' and he would smash one in from the corner flag.

"I'm really proud of him. He has done a lot better than a lot of people would have expected but not us. If his attitude had anything to do with it, he was always going to make it to the top."

Kane's first introduction to the world of professional football came in 2001, when he was invited to join Arsenal's youth academy. The following year, the forward was released by the club – with Kane still remembering to this day the news that he was being let go by the Gunners.

"So, one day when I was eight years old, I was walking to the park with my dad, and he said, right out of the blue, 'I've got to tell you something," recalled Kane on *The Players' Tribune*. "I said, 'Yeah, what is it?' Then I remember he put his arm around my shoulder, and he said, Well, Harry… Arsenal have released you.'

"I can't really recall what I felt in that moment. To be honest — I don't even think I really knew what it meant. I was too young. But I do remember how my father reacted, and how it made me feel. He didn't criticise me. He didn't criticise Arsenal. He didn't even look especially bothered by it at all. He just said, 'Don't worry, Harry. We'll work harder — and we'll go on and we'll find another club, alright?'

In the weeks leading up to his first North London derby in February 2015, images of Harry wearing an Arsenal kit during his year-long spell with the Gunners mischievously emerged. Rival supporters took to social media to question Kane's footballing loyalties. The striker was quick to set the record straight "I wanted to wear a Tottenham kit but I don't think that would've gone down too well," Kane told Spurs TV in the run-up to the match. "I was eight years-old. I was at Arsenal for a year and obviously I was a kid, I just wanted to play football.

Kane would have the last laugh in the game, scoring twice as Spurs went on to beat Arsenal 2-1 at White Hart Lane, having trailed to an early strike from Mezut Ozil. After the game, he commented:

"Of course, it was nice to score after that picture. I'm Tottenham through and through and this (his performance and celebration against the Gunners that afternoon) shows that. It was an emotional day and one I was very pleased with. Most of my family were Spurs fans and I grew up 15 minutes from the ground, so I was always going to be a Spurs fan".

Harry went to Spurs matches with his father from an early age. He also followed the England national team as a youngster, with his first memories of a World Cup dating back to the Three Lions' appearance at the 2002 tournament in Japan and South Korea.

"The Brazil game (at that tournament) sticks out," Kane told the Football Association website in an interview prior to his own appearance at the World Cup in 2018. "We went 1-0 up but Brazil managed to turn it around. Because of the time difference in Japan, we got to watch it in the assembly hall at school. It wasn't a great day afterwards!

"David Beckham's penalty against Argentina in 2002 is a definite highlight. My Tottenham boss Mauricio Pochettino was obviously the player who gave away the penalty (by bringing down Michael Owen) so we have a bit of banter about it every now and then. I was a big Beckham fan growing up, obviously it's well known that he's from the same area and we went to the same school. To see the passion in his eyes after he scored that penalty is something that sticks out. In 2006, I watched the Portugal game in the Sirloin pub in Chingford with my family. There were a few tears at the end of that game."

Harry's favourite Spurs player growing up was Teddy Sheringham – who was raised locally to Kane in Highams Park. Sheringham spent two spells at Tottenham during his career and was the club's top Premier League goal scorer for many years – with 97 strikes – prior to Kane breaking his record in January 2018.

The comparisons between Kane and Sheringham have existed throughout Harry's career to date. In an interview with talkSPORT in 2014, Harry Redknapp – who managed Sheringham at Portsmouth and Kane at Spurs – said of the current England captain: "He's a little bit in the Teddy Sheringham mould. He hasn't got great pace but he is a clever, clever player and technically he is very good. He is a bit like Teddy with that sharp mind. He's a fantastic footballer, he's got a great attitude and you couldn't meet a nicer lad."

Kane got the opportunity to talk to his Spurs idol for the first time at a charity golf day shortly after his loan spell at Millwall – another of Sheringham's former clubs – ended in 2012.

"It was great to meet him," Kane told the Press Association. "I was a little bit star-struck, to be honest. When you meet your idol you don't really know what to say but he had great conversation. As I grew up, I tried to use him as a role model and if I can score as many goals as he did, it would not be bad. He's a great finisher and was very good at getting in the box and scoring so many goals for Spurs."

When he was a Year 7 pupil at Chingford Foundation School, Harry had a chance meeting with another of his Spurs heroes when the club's striker Jermain Defoe spotted him and a group of friends playing football on the street and stopped his car.

"This black Range Rover turned up and Jermain Defoe just got out and started playing football with us," Kane told presenter Clare Balding on her BT Sport show. "I was only 11 or 12 at the time so that was mental. It was great for him to do it and I spoke to him about it while he was at the club and he remembers it. That's definitely a memory I won't forget."

Kane's biggest highlight following Spurs as a youngster meanwhile came on February 24, 2008, when he was at Wembley Stadium to see the Lilywhites beat Chelsea 2-1 in the League Cup Final.

"The final stands out for me because I was there as a fan and with my family," Kane told *The Guardian* on the eve of his own appearance for Spurs in a League Cup Final against Chelsea in 2015. "To see them lift the trophy and all the fans to stay behind and to stay with them is something that I've been thinking of leading up to this final."

Harry's closeness to his family and the support they have given him over the years was a re-occurring theme during the writing of this book. In the previously discussed *Daily Mirror* article on his grandad Eric, Harry's great aunt Bette said his parents have always been there for him.

"You'd be at the house and this little boy would come in, with all his knees dirty, Kim would have the kit straight in the wash," recalled Bette. "If Harry should thank anyone it should be his mum and his dad. He could not have better parents. I told Kim last time I saw her – 'your dad would be so proud'."

Kane has himself acknowledged the role his parents have played in shaping his life and his career in an interview with *The Sun*.

"My mum and dad helped me get to this stage, taking me training every night and putting in the hard work behind the scenes," he said. "I owe a lot to my family, we're a strong unit."

Chris Ramsey – who worked with Kane throughout his development at Tottenham Hotspur from Under-12 to first-team level and who has offered his exclusive thoughts on Harry for this book – is also full of praise for the role his family have played in shaping his career.

"He has been brought up very well by his parents," acknowledged Ramsey. "First and foremost, Harry is a lovely lad with no airs and graces. If he came into my office right now, we'd just be sitting down having a cup of tea and talking like I saw him yesterday. He is very generous with his time and very polite. Credit has to go to Harry and the way he was raised for that.

"As well as having supportive parents, he's close to his brother and he's got the same girlfriend he's had since leaving school. Harry is a super role model and I really can't talk any more highly about him."

Those who attend Spurs or England matches will likely have spotted Harry's family in the crowd – with Pat, Kim and Charlie regular match-goers, along with his fiancée Katie Goodland. Kim said of her son in a rare interview; "We just want him to keep doing what he's doing. We are all football fans and a football family. We spend every weekend watching Harry, going round the country to see him."

Ahead of the 2018 FIFA World Cup, Charlie expressed his pride in his younger brother being named captain of England, Tweeting:

"Proud brother post alert!!!… From playing over Ridgeway Park to watching England down the Sirloin pub, this is the ultimate dream come true. Well done little bro and good luck #comeonengland #russia #worldcup #captain." @CharlieKane123 – May 22, 2018.

Harry's pathway to eventually becoming a Premier League star and England captain had an uncertain beginning. After he was released by Arsenal in 2002, he attended a trial at his beloved Tottenham Hotspur, but didn't make the grade at the time. He then joined Watford for a trial period in 2004, during which time he lined up for them in a schoolboy match against Spurs that seemingly reignited the possibility of Kane signing for 'his' club.

"It's funny how things work out — as it was after playing for Watford against Tottenham that I got the opportunity to join Tottenham's youth academy," Kane told *The Players' Tribune*. "The white kit fit (sic) better on me, I think."

Kane left Watford and became part of Tottenham's youth set-up in 2004, the same year in which Chris Ramsey joined the club as Assistant Academy Manager. Ramsey still remembers his first encounters with an 11-year-old Harry Kane.

"There is no sensational story about his (Kane's) early days," admitted Ramsey, who also held a role as Head of Player Development (Under-9-16s) while Kane was in Tottenham's academy. "In those days, there was certainly no real signs that he would be where he is in the game today. In fact, there were a lot of factors that were against him in those early days… its well-known that he was a late developer in terms of his physicality. Technically though, he was very good. Myself and (Spurs Academy Manager from May 2005) John McDermott always put a real emphasis on technical players at Spurs and his ability from that point of view was one of his prevailing strengths. It allowed him to progress through the academy system at the club.

"What also struck me about Harry very early on was his mental strength. There was a determination to succeed and he always showed a willingness to work on his technique and to keep improving."

Kane played a midfield role when he originally joined Spurs before adapting to become a striker. He drew further comparisons with Teddy Sheringham in the Tottenham Academy, as he took on the deep-lying forward role – the classic 'number ten' – occupied by Sheringham during his playing days.

"Because of the way we played, most of the players in the academy had to have certain midfield attributes," explained Ramsey. "Harry started out as a midfielder and as he developed as a forward, he was still immensely comfortable dropping into midfield to play. Harry played as a 'number ten' as often as he did as a 'number nine' and to be honest, he could do an equally good job as a 'number eight', a 'number four' etc. Some of his passing is unbelievable… He can work back and play and sit in there. He can head it, he can pass it. What I'm getting at here is the fact that Harry is a great all-round footballer, which is not always the case with 'number nines'. He's a magnificent, technical player that just happens to have the canny knack of scoring goal after goal too!"

A year on from joining Spurs' youth set-up Kane attended the launch of the now-defunct David Beckham Academy in Greenwich and stood next to the then-England captain in a group photograph with 15 other young footballers. "Just to be in his (Beckham's) presence was an honour… hopefully I will meet him again one day soon," said Kane in 2015. To Beckham's right in the photograph was Harry's friend from Chingford Foundation School and now fiancée, Kate Goodland, who gave birth to their daughter Ivy in January 2017 with their second child due in the summer of 2018.

Kane played a major role in the success of his Chingford Foundation School football team. As a Year 10 pupil, he was part of their side which won a cup competition at Brisbane Road – the same venue where Harry would play many of his early matches as a professional on loan at Leyton Orient.

The side became known as the 'Harry Kane Team' – as the trophies rolled in and Harry banged in the goals left, right and centre. The player featured in fewer matches for them in his final year of studies though, as an academy contract with Spurs loomed. He missed a number of games en route to the Borough Cup Final in 2009. Despite manager

Mark Leadon wanting him to play in that final, Harry felt his place in the side belonged to the player that had replaced him in the line-up in the previous matches.

"By Year 11 we managed his time more," explained Leadon in a BBC feature on Kane. "Because we knew he was going to sign for Tottenham, we only played him in the big games – County Cup, Essex and London cups. We played without him in the Borough Cup, but we got to the final and were going to play our strongest team with Harry. He came to us and said he didn't think it was right, please could he be a sub, because the guy in his place had done really well."

During his school days he also represented Essex' county team prior to the magical day on July 28, 2009 – Kane's 16th birthday – when he became a Spurs Academy Scholar. His journey to that point had been far from straightforward, with members of Tottenham's academy staff acknowledging there were points along his development path where other clubs could – and probably would – have released him.

"If you were to look at his stature when he was an Under-15 for example, I can imagine many clubs would have let him go at that stage, based on his physicality," comments Ramsey. "Tottenham as a club have to be commended for their patience in their youth system to allow players like him to go on and achieve."

In his first season with Spurs' Under-18s in 2008-09, Kane was selected to compete in the Copa Chivas and Bellinzona tournaments, scoring three times in the former in Mexico. His FA Premier Academy League debut was as a substitute in a 4-2 victory over Leicester City in March 2009. His first goal in the league came on his inaugural start in a 4-1 win against West Ham United a few months later.

The following season saw Kane become a regular for the Spurs Under-18 side, netting 18 times in 22 league fixtures, that included a hat-trick in an 8-1 demolition of Coventry City.

His prolific form in front of goal brought him to the attention of the club's first-team manager at the time, Harry Redknapp. He gave the youngster his first taste of senior action by naming him on the bench for a League Cup game against Everton and an FA Cup tie with Bolton Wanderers during the 2009-10 campaign.

Spurs had an international role call of first-team strikers at that time with the likes of Peter Crouch, Jermain Defoe, Robbie Keane and Roman Pavlyuchenko, while Icelandic frontman Eidur Gudjohnsen signed on loan during the season. Dutch international Rafael van der Vaart was to arrive from Real Madrid in August 2010 while a certain Gareth Bale was starting to show that he was better suited to an advanced role at the club who had originally signed him as a left-back. With such an array of attacking talent at White Hart Lane, Harry had quite a battle on his hands to forge a place in the first-team.

CHAPTER FIVE

HERE, THERE AND EVERYWHERE

Harry Kane's goal scoring form for the Spurs Under-18 side saw him receive his first international call-up in January 2010 as he was named in the England Under-17 squad for the Algarve Tournament.

He was joined by the likes of Ross Barkley, Jack Butland, Benik Afobe and Saido Berahino, who have gone on to establish themselves as household names. The Tottenham striker made his debut for John Peacock's side in their 1-1 draw with France at the age of 16 years and 200 days which was followed by a substitute appearance against the Ukraine. The Three Lions' goalless draw with hosts Portugal on the final day of the competition was enough to see them crowned as tournament winners.

Harry returned to the squad in March 2010 for a series of qualifying matches for the UEFA Under-17 European Championships. The 'elite round' of fixtures had a tournament feel to them, with the four-teams in Group 7 – England, Sweden, Malta and Slovakia – all going head-to-head in the space of six days. The group winners plus the best-placed runners-up achieved qualification to the championships hosted in Liechtenstein a few months later.

Kane played in England's three matches, scoring a penalty in the 5-0 win over Malta while he also netted in the 2-0 victory against Slovakia as the young Three Lions made it through to the finals. Illness denied Harry the opportunity to feature at the championships in May 2010 – Peacock's youngsters went on to triumph in his absence, winning the competition for the first time.

Despite the disappointment of missing out in Liechtenstein, it had still been a great 2009-10 season for Kane, who captained the Spurs Under-18 side and made it onto the bench for two first-team fixtures. Harry made the step up to England Under-19 level the following campaign, scoring twice on his debut in a 6-1 triumph over Albania in October 2010.

With Kane impressing at youth level for club and country, the possibility of letting him go out on loan to a Football League club was discussed by then-Tottenham manager Harry Redknapp and his academy staff: "At that time, he needed that experience of first-team football and we had senior players ahead of him," explained Redknapp. In January 2011, then-League One club Leyton Orient secured his services until the end of the season.

On January 15, 2011, the striker made his professional debut for the O's, coming on as a 73rd minute substitute for Scott McGleish in a 1-1 draw at Rochdale. Paul Levy and Steve Nussbaum from the *Orient Outlook Podcast* (soundcloud.com/orient-outlook) recalled their early memories of watching Kane and other Spurs loanees Tom Carroll and Paul-Jose Mpoku;

"He was a tall, baby faced striker that came with a good reputation and Spurs don't send their promising youngsters just anywhere for their development. We thought 'they (Kane, Carroll and Mpoku) must be ones for the future'."

A week after Orient's trip to Spotland, Kane was handed his first start for the club as Russell Slade's men hosted Sheffield Wednesday on January 22. Harry marked the occasion with a goal, getting on the end of a Dean Cox free-kick to put the O's two up in a game they won 4-0. The following month, the number 29 came off the bench to score twice in a 4-1 victory over Bristol Rovers during a loan spell that would yield five goals in 18 matches for the East End club overall.

"Despite Harry's goal return, I thought he would end up being released by Spurs and get a contract at a lower league club, which is the journey many Premier League youth players take," added Levy and Nussbaum. "What a difference seven years make eh?!"

While Kane's overall experience of Leyton Orient was a positive one, there were disappointments along the way too. He was an unused substitute in the club's 1-1 draw with Arsenal in the fifth round of the FA Cup – a fixture he admitted was "extra-special for me being a Spurs player" – while he was suspended for the replay at the Emirates. He also received the first red card of his senior career at Huddersfield in February 2011 – not long after coming off the bench to score in a 2-2 draw.

"I got a yellow early," Kane told the *Daily Mail*, explaining his sending off. "Then later this guy kicked into me and fell over and rolled around. The home fans got into it and I was sent off. The guy knew exactly what he was doing. He was being smart and I wasn't. The worst thing was we had Arsenal in an FA Cup replay next and I missed that. I was gutted. So there we go. Lesson learned."

Orient finished seventh in the League One table in 2010-11, missing out on a play-off spot by a single point. Over at White Hart Lane, Spurs competed in the UEFA Champions League for the first time – reaching the quarter-final stage – and came fifth in the Premier League. Kane returned to N17 that summer, as the Lilywhites got the new season underway with a 5-0 win at Scottish side Heart of Midlothian in the UEFA Europa League.

Confident they had already done enough to win the two-legged play-off tie, Spurs manager Harry Redknapp made nine changes to his team for the return match at White Hart Lane. Only Michael Dawson and Jake Livermore retained their places from the original game in Edinburgh while Tottenham debuts were handed to a number of the club's academy graduates, including Tom Carroll and Ryan Fredericks.

Kane was given the news he had longed for, as he too was included on Redknapp's list of starters. Harry wore the number 37 shirt on his Lilywhites' debut, playing the full 90 minutes upfront alongside Russian international Roman Pavlyuchenko. One of Harry's Spurs heroes, Jermain Defoe, watched from the bench as the lad he'd once had a kick-about with in the street was now in first-team action for Tottenham.

"It was great to have the opportunity to give several youngsters the chance to play that night," said Redknapp. "In terms of Harry, he was one of a number of young players at that time we thought had a decent chance of becoming a Premier League footballer."

In all, six players in the squad to face Hearts that evening had come through the club's academy – Kane, Livermore, Carroll, Fredericks, Jake Nicholson and Andros Townsend. None of the youngsters looked over-awed by the occasion of playing a European tie in front of a crowd of nearly 25,000. Indeed, it was two of the young debutants who combined to fashion the best chance of the first-half. Carroll's weighted pass sent Kane through one-on-one with Hearts goalkeeper Jamie MacDonald who clipped him.

A penalty was awarded and it was Harry – rather than the established Russian international striker Pavlyuchenko – who stepped up to take the spot-kick. Alas, he was to denied a debut goal for Spurs, as MacDonald made a good save. "I can't remember what I said to him after that game, but I'm sure I'd have told him not to worry," reflected Redknapp on Kane's penalty miss. "It's just one of those things. He had the confidence to take the penalty in the first place, which tells you all you need to know about Harry's character."

Kane offered his own thoughts on the penalty to Spurs TV: "I waited for the keeper to dive, he went one way and then dived the other and unfortunately saved it. He's fooled me and I'll hold my hands up to that. But obviously I'll learn from that, these things happen and I'll be ready to take the next one if it happens again, I'm that sort of player."

Daniel Wynne – a lifelong Tottenham Hotspur supporter and the club's matchday commentator – watched Kane's debut, which finished in a goalless draw, securing Tottenham's passage to the group stage of the Europa League.

"I remember Harry's debut very well," said Wynne, who has worked for the club since 2001. "I had heard a lot about Harry Kane (prior to the game) and had seen him a few times. He was well thought of and big things were expected. He had only just turned 18 the previous month and it was one of those lovely stories of a local lad progressing through the ranks to play in the first team.

"Every fan thinks they can spot a talented youngster and whilst everyone got behind him that night, I left the ground feeling underwhelmed. He looked a little chubby, slow and his first touch looked suspect. I remember watching Wayne Rooney as a 16-year-old playing at White Hart Lane in the FA Youth Cup and he stood out as he stole the show. I didn't feel the same when I saw Harry. He missed a penalty too which I thought would have a massive negative impact for an 18-year-old on his debut. I confess to wondering whether he would be able to bounce back from that."

Chris Ramsey, Harry's former coach, didn't share those concerns: "I can imagine the next penalty Harry took was probably placed in a similar position to the one against Hearts, just better executed," smiled Ramsey. "That's the thing with Harry, it was always about improvement. He would have been thinking after that penalty against Hearts 'I did the right thing, I just didn't execute it properly' and off he would have gone to practice penalties."

With Redknapp often rotating his squad for Europa League matches, Kane got a number of opportunities to feature for Spurs. He started the opening Group A fixture that campaign as the Lilywhites drew 0-0 away to Greek side PAOK and came on as a substitute in matches with Shamrock Rovers (home) and Rubin Kazan (away).

"His performances in the Europa League just confirmed what I'd always thought about Harry, that he was a good young player with the ability to one day go on and play in the Premier League," commented Redknapp. "He wasn't a player you look at in the same way I did at Joe Cole aged 11, who was a genius and you knew without doubt was going to be a star. Harry was more like a Frank Lampard… someone who worked and worked to get where he wanted."

A great personal moment for Harry came on November 30, 2011 as he started up front alongside Spurs idol Jermain Defoe for the first time in a 2-1 defeat to PAOK at White Hart Lane. The Lilywhites bowed out of Europe, despite a 4-0 victory over Shamrock Rovers in their final group game. The night marked another landmark for Kane, who scored his first goal for Tottenham as Daniel Wynne recalled: "He came on as a sub with about 15 minutes to play and he got on the end of a loose ball in the six-yard box, turned and rifled it home."

Harry featured in six European matches for Spurs in the first-half of the 2011-12 season but was yet to be handed his Premier League debut. Robbie Keane departed White Hart Lane in the summer of 2011 and was replaced by former Arsenal frontman Emmanuel Adebayor. French forward Louis Saha was also recruited that campaign, as the club maintained a healthy base of attacking options.

Towards the end of 2011, Championship side Millwall expressed an interest in taking Kane and Tottenham team mate Ryan Mason on loan and the pair headed to South London early in the new year. George Lampey, a Lions supporter for over 50 years and one of the hosts of the podcast *No One Likes Us Talkin!* (www.noonelikesustalkin. com) was impressed with the striker's progress at The Den.

"Harry was a raw young talent from the Premiership and we needed someone to help us score goals to retain our Championship status," said Lampey. "In an FA Cup clash with Dagenham and Redbridge, his two goals of our five showed his potential and his performance brought some hope when we were struggling at the wrong end of the table.

"It was very noticeable how Harry grew into a better player as his time with us progressed. After his two FA Cup goals, he went on a run of six games without scoring but despite that it was clear his skills were positively contributing to the team's improvement.

"His eventual run of scoring seven goals in fourteen games plus his assists were above and beyond someone of his age. I remember our replay in the FA Cup at Southampton, they were in amongst the promotion contenders in the Championship and we were at the other end. Harry's overall influence in that game was outstanding and enabled us to come back from being 2–1 down to winning by the odd goal in five. He had two assists in that game, his stature grew and grew and the second assist from a repeated one-two with Trotter who scored the winner showed that Harry was going to be something special.

"Another fine display at Doncaster was capped by him scoring a wonder goal from 35-yards out from a Jimmy Abdou pass. But probably the goal that won the hearts and minds of Millwall fans most was at Portsmouth, who were and still are fierce adversaries. They too were at the wrong end of the table and Harry fired what has become a trademark shot from just outside the area into the bottom corner of the net, which brought all three points back to South East London.

"His final game for us was against Play-Off challenging Blackpool at The Den and although we had secured our Championship status, this team – inspired by the young but gutsy Harry Kane – were not going to sit back on their laurels. Despite some great play, the Lions were 2–1 down when a corner was only half-cleared to Kane on the edge of the box and he rifled another trademark finish into the bottom-left corner. Hero status was attained and the team finished being unbeaten in seven matches to end the season. Interestingly, we never lost when Harry scored."

Such was Kane's impact at Millwall he was named as the club's Young Player of the Year. "He was deserving (of the club's award) as he played a pivotal role in us staying up," said Lampey.

Manager Kenny Jackett commented on the Lions' official website, "He has fitted in very well at Millwall despite only being here half a season. He's fitted in with the players and the crowd and developed as well. I felt he came here as a boy and is a man now – and plays like a man on the pitch. It's been a good relationship and he deserves the award."

Kane left Millwall having secured the affections of The Den faithful but Chris Ramsey recalls an early trip to watch the striker in SE16 when he was still to win some of the club's fans around;

"Myself, Les (Ferdinand) and Tim (Sherwood) would take it in turns to go and see Harry play when he was on loan and would write reports on the games," said Ramsey. "I remember going to watch Harry at Millwall when Ryan Mason was playing there. I remember hearing comments in the crowd like 'at Tottenham they might have some good players but Harry Kane's not ready'. X amount of years on, the persistence of the boy to not be beat – his willingness to work hard and practice all the time – is just incredible. He went from four loan spells to being named the tenth best player in the world in the Ballon d'Or."

In the run-up to the 2012-13 season, Kane scored a hat-trick in a 6-0 victory for a Spurs development side against Southend United at the club's training centre, Hotspur Way. He was included in the first-team squad for the Lilywhites' trip to Newcastle United on the opening weekend of the Premier League campaign and made his top-flight debut in that fixture, coming on as an 86th minute substitution for Sandro.

Thoughts of Kane gaining a regular first-team berth under new Spurs manager Andre Villas-Boas were short lived as the striker was loaned to Norwich City just a few weeks later. Prior to his move to Norfolk, Harry joined up with the England Under-21 squad for the first time, having been selected by then-manager Stuart Pearce. He was an unused substitute in the Three Lions' 1-0 victory over Norway at Chesterfield's Proact Stadium on September 10.

Five days later, Kane replaced Grant Holt as a 71st minute substitute to make his Norwich City debut in the Canaries' goalless draw with West Ham United. Harry had two chances to win the game late on but couldn't find the breakthrough goal. Norwich boss and former Spurs player Chris Hughton commented: "Harry Kane will learn a lot from this experience. I think he will be a super player."

In his next appearance and first start for Norwich – a 1-0 League Cup victory over Doncaster Rovers on September 26 – Kane suffered a broken metatarsal. The injury dashed his hopes of being included in England's squad for their UEFA European Under-21 Championship qualification play-off with Serbia. He returned to Tottenham during a two-month spell on the side-lines, with the club's medical team aiding his rehabilitation.

Harry headed back to Norwich in December and came on as a substitute in the Canaries' 4-3 defeat to Manchester City that month. He also featured in a Premier League match against West Ham United and an FA Cup tie with Luton Town. Kane was expected to spend the rest of the 2012-13 season at Carrow Road but was recalled early by his parent club during the January transfer window.

Just weeks after the young striker started training with Spurs again, Millwall made an approach to re-sign Harry on loan but Tottenham decided to send him to fellow Championship club Leicester City instead. Just 20 days after his return from Norwich,

Kane was now a Foxes' player. At that time, it was also announced that he had signed a new contract at White Hart Lane, running until 2017.

"We didn't know a lot about him (Kane)," reflected *Leicester Mercury's* Robert Tanner, who has been covering the Foxes since 2009 and was introduced to Kane shortly after he arrived at the club: "In those days City would let us interview players down at the training ground. I met Harry before his debut at Blackpool (February 23, 2013) and he was very similar to how he was now. He was eloquent and mature for his age. He had obviously been media trained at Spurs and came across as ambitious, desperate to play and prove himself.

"There was some uncertainty about what his best position was and (then-Leicester manager) Nigel Pearson said he could play anywhere across the front line, and if memory serves me right he played on the right flank on his debut."

Kane made 15 appearances and scored twice for Leicester during the closing months of the season, that saw the Foxes reach the Championship play-off semi-finals. Despite netting on his home debut in a 3-0 win over Blackburn Rovers, the striker endured a tough time at the King Power Stadium.

"He started his first five games but Pearson then used him only as a substitute for the rest of the season," recalled Tanner. "David Nugent came back into the side and started scoring a few goals, and his partnership with Chris Wood blossomed as City reached the play-offs. There is a famous photograph of Kane, Jamie Vardy and Danny Drinkwater – three future England internationals – watching from the substitutes' bench during the dramatic 3–1 play-off semi-final defeat at Watford (May 12, 2013). He came on in that game."

Whilst out on loan to various different clubs, Kane's international progress continued, as he played a key role in England reaching the semi-finals of the UEFA European Under-19 Championships in 2012. In all, he made 14 appearances for the side, scoring six goals. He made his England Under-20 debut against Uruguay on June 23, 2013 before starting in the Three Lions' 2-2 draw with Iraq at the FIFA Under-20 World Cup a week later. His first goal at the tournament came three days later as Peter Taylor's team drew 1-1 with Chile. Defeat to Egypt in the final Group E game saw a squad – also including the likes of John Stones, Ross Barkley and Eric Dier – eliminated.

Chris Ramsey travelled to the tournament in Turkey, which was won by France. "That (England) team was ultimately unsuccessful considering the players we had," commented Ramsey. "Harry got criticism for the fact we didn't do as well as we should have done and he didn't score the goals. Did that faze him? No. It just wasn't his or the team's moment."

For all the ups and downs of his various loan moves, Harry was philosophical when he spoke to the Football Association's official website about his early career. "I had setbacks, plenty of them, but I always had belief that I was going to get to where I wanted to be and that was playing for Tottenham and then England," said Kane.

"Even when I went out on loan to the clubs, it was always to come back and become a Spurs player. I had good loan spells at Leyton Orient and Millwall and not such a good loan with Norwich City and Leicester City. That is all part of the learning curve. There are blips in any career, but that is part of football and it is how you deal with it and I think I've dealt with it quite well. I'm sure there will be more times when I have setbacks in my career, but it's about how you can move forward (from them). I think self-belief is massive. If you don't believe in yourself, not many others will. Work hard and believe in yourself and you will go as far as your body will take you."

Harry Redknapp, who sanctioned Kane's moves to Orient and Millwall believed his time away from White Hart Lane did him "the world of good". "The loan system is one I've always believed in and I sent the likes of Rio Ferdinand, Joe Cole, Frank Lampard, Michael Carrick, Jermain Defoe etc out on loan to lower division clubs when I managed them at West Ham" he said. "I'm sure those loans were a great experience for Harry. He did really well at Leyton Orient and Millwall, Norwich he had his injury and obviously Leicester was a bit more difficult because he didn't play that many games. The loans were still much better for him at that age than playing Under-21 football in my opinion."

Chris Ramsey is also of the belief that Harry's loans have helped shape the career of the world-class player we see today. "There was negativity during some of those loan moves but what he did was to grab on to that and turn it into a positive" added Ramsey. "People were saying on some of those loans, 'he's slow, he can't do this, he can't do that'. He responded by saying to himself 'actually, I'm not slow, I can do this and I can do that... now I'm going to work hard, listen to the people that matter and prove the doubters wrong'.

"When he came back from the fourth loan, the possibility of him going out (on loan) again was mooted, Harry spoke to Tim (Sherwood), Les Ferdinand and myself and almost bullied us into staying at Spurs, telling us he didn't want to go elsewhere. He had the confidence to believe he could be better than the first-team players in his position that had cost ten, 20 and 30 million."

Kane's steely determination and belief on the back of his four loans suggested he was in the right place mentally to compete for a first-team place at White Hart Lane heading into the 2013-14 season. An upcoming managerial change in N17 was about to help the forward stake his claim...

CHAPTER SIX

NEW BEGINNINGS

From a Tottenham Hotspur perspective, the summer of 2013 was dominated by talk of the possible departure of the club's star player, Gareth Bale. It seemed a case of business as usual when the Welsh wizard fired Spurs ahead in a 1-1 draw at Swindon Town in a pre-season friendly on July 16, 2013. But the reigning PFA Player of the Year's appearance at the County Ground was to prove to be his last for Spurs. He was left out of the squad that travelled to Colchester United three days later and subsequently completed a then-world record transfer to Real Madrid on September 1.

As Bale was preparing to leave Tottenham Hotspur, a Spurs youngster was trying hard to stake his claim for regular inclusion in the club's first-team squad. Harry Kane featured as a second-half replacement for Emmanuel Adebayor in Spurs' goalless draw at Colchester. Of the 9,988 crowd present that evening, who could have imagined that the 19-year-old substitute would one day be mentioned in the same 'world class' category as Bale?!

Kane played and scored in Tottenham's 5-2 friendly defeat at AS Monaco on August 3 before returning to Under-21 Premier League duties for the club nine days later. He was on the scoresheet as the Spurs youngsters beat their Chelsea counterparts 4-2 and a busy start to the season continued for the striker, as he was called-up to England's Under-21 squad. It was the nation's senior manager Roy Hodgson – in temporary charge of the Under-21s – who handed Harry his debut as he came on as a 58th minute substitute for Connor Wickham in a 6-0 victory over Scotland at Bramall Lane.

After scoring a hat-trick for Tottenham in a 6-3 victory over Manchester City in the Under-21 Premier League, Kane was rewarded with a place in the first-team squad for the Europa League matches with Georgian outfit Dinamo Tbilisi. He got some valuable playing time in both legs of the play-off tie, coming on as a substitute for new signing Roberto Soldado in the first game and

Andros Townsend in the second. Spurs progressed comfortably to the group stages of the competition with an 8-0 aggregate win.

The summer transfer window closed on September 2, ending a busy few months for those responsible for player recruitment at Tottenham Hotspur. Bale's departure from the club prompted a major rebuilding exercise with Paulinho, Nacer Chadli, Roberto Soldado, Etienne Capoue, Vlad Chiriches, Christian Eriksen and Erik Lamela brought to White Hart Lane. With manager Andre Villas-Boas favouring a 4-2-3-1 formation and having strikers such as Emmanual Adebayor, Jermain Defoe and now Soldado on his books, Kane had a real battle on his hands to keep himself in contention for a place in the first-team squad.

After Kane's appearances against Dinamo Tbilisi, his next first-team involvement also came in the Europa League as he was an unused substitute for the 3-0 victory over Tromso IL in September. His first taste of Premier League action that season came in a 1-0 win at Cardiff City. He took his place in the starting line-up as the Lilywhites triumphed 4-0 at Aston Villa in the League Cup while he was an unused substitute in Tottenham's 2-0 win at FC Anji in the Europa League a few weeks later.

On October 3, Kane was selected as part of an attack-minded England Under-21 squad for the upcoming European qualifiers against San Marino and Lithuania, joining the likes of Tom Ince, Raheem Sterling, Wilfred Zaha, Saido Berahino and Ravel Morrison. He was handed his first start for the Under-21s against San Marino by newly appointed manager Gareth Southgate. Harry quickly became a prolific goal scorer at that level, with eight goals in 14 appearances which included a hat-trick in the 4-0 victory in San Marino that month.

"Before the game, I was aiming for a hat-trick and I got a hat-trick," Kane told FATV after the match against one of European football's smallest nations. "As a striker, you want to be scoring as many goals as you can. It feels good and I'm very pleased."

Manager Gareth Southgate was delighted by Kane's display and added: "It is always memorable to score a hat-trick for your country and he (Kane) should be very proud of that. He had some good service. There are things that we can take from this. All you can do is try to do the right thing and keep learning."

After his hat-trick heroics for England's Under-21s against San Marino, Kane took his place on the bench for the match with Lithuania at Portman Road. He was an unused substitute in the 5-0 victory, that saw Ravel Morrison and Saido Berahino bag braces while James Ward-Prowse was also on target.

On his return from international duties, Harry's next involvement in the Tottenham first-team came as a 78th minute substitute in the Lilywhites' League Cup fourth round tie with Hull City. The match headed into extra-time after a 1-1 draw in the 90 minutes. The Lilywhites went behind in the added period, before Kane made it 2-2 with a low shot past Eldin Jakupovic. The ensuing penalty shootout required 18 spot-kicks to settle the result with Spurs running out eventual 8-7 winners.

"It was a bizarre night," reflected Spurs TV commentator Daniel Wynne. "Erik Lamela had missed for us by the time Harry stepped up to take the last of the regulation five penalties. I remember thinking it was a big test given how he had missed one on his debut. But he stood up to the task and converted his spot kick. (Spurs goalkeeper) Brad Friedel grabbed the headlines as he saved twice in the shootout but Harry left an impression on me that night with his composure and bravery in taking what could have been the decisive penalty."

Harry made his third substitute appearance in the Europa League that season in the Lilywhites' 2-1 home victory over Sheriff

Tiraspol. That evening, Jermain Defoe scored a club-record 23rd European goal for the Lilywhites, surpassing the tally of club legend Martin Chivers. Kane replaced Gylfi Sigurdsson in the second half of that game, coming on just two minutes after Defoe had broken the record with a firmly struck penalty. Erik Lamela also scored in the game which confirmed Tottenham's place in the knockout phase of the competition.

Shortly after, Kane withdrew from the England Under-21 squad for matches with Finland and San Marino having sustained a back injury. He didn't feature in the Spurs first-team squad again until New Year's Day 2014, when he came on as a substitute for Roberto Soldado in Spurs' 2-1 triumph at Manchester United. The occasion marked the club's first-ever back-to-back victory at Old Trafford in the Premier League.

During Kane's spell on the side-lines, a 5-0 loss to Liverpool in December 2013 – the club's heaviest home defeat in the Premier League in some 16 years – saw manager Andre Villas-Boas depart White Hart Lane after 18 months in charge. A host of names were linked to the vacancy in the tabloids, with ex-England boss Fabio Capello, Champions League-winning manager Roberto Di Matteo, Swansea's Michael Laudrup and the club's then-Technical Director Franco Baldini mentioned in dispatches along with Lilywhites legend Glenn Hoddle.

On December 16, it was announced that three individuals who had been key to Kane's development in the Spurs academy would assume first-team coaching duties on a temporary basis. Tim Sherwood became Caretaker Manager with Chris Ramsey and Les Ferdinand appointed as First-Team Coaches.

Given Sherwood's past roles as Technical Co-ordinator and Head of Football Development within the Spurs academy, the new boss was well aware of the talent that lay throughout the club's ranks. He named two academy graduates as substitutes for his first game in charge against West Ham United in the League Cup on December 18 as Ryan Fredericks and Zeki Fryers took their place on the bench. Fryers came on for Danny Rose in the 2-1 defeat. Fredericks was also in the squad for Spurs' visit to Southampton in the Premier League four days later in a match that saw fellow youth product Nabil Bentaleb make his professional debut as a replacement for Mousa Dembele in the 3-2 victory.

"It wasn't like we (Sherwood, Ferdinand and Ramsey) took on our roles thinking we were going to drop all the first-team players and promote all the academy players," commented Ferdinand on the opportunities handed to Spurs' youngsters during Tim Sherwood's managerial reign. "Each and every player is selected on merit. Of the youngsters that played early on, Bentaleb was one of the first.

"All managers will say to you that when they pick a team, they do so on the basis of selecting the players they trust. Everyone can have a bad game, but you always know of the individuals in your ranks – 'one will do this, one will do that'. Tim knew of the particular qualities we needed in certain areas at the time and Bentaleb was one of those players he knew he could trust."

After his first two matches in temporary charge, Sherwood was handed the managerial role at White Hart Lane on a permanent basis, signing an 18-month contract. His side drew 1-1 at home to West Bromwich Albion days later. Kane's return to the first-team at Manchester United on New Year's Day 2014 was followed by his inclusion in the squad for a trip to Arsenal three days later. The striker was an unused substitute in the Lilywhites' FA Cup third round tie at the Emirates Stadium. Harry's last match of the month came in the Under-21 Premier League, as he scored in a 4-1 win over Newcastle United at Hotspur Way.

Kane divided his time between the first-team and under-21s throughout February 2014, starting the month by making a substitute appearance in a 1-1 draw at Hull City in the Premier League. He also featured as a substitute in both legs of the Europa League round of 32 tie with Dnipro while he remained on the bench for league games at Newcastle United and Norwich City that month. In between, he started in the Lilywhites' Under-21 Premier League fixtures against Everton and Bolton Wanderers.

On March 2, Roberto Soldado scored just his second Premier League goal from open play for Spurs in a 1-0 win over Cardiff City during a struggling season for the Spanish striker. Kane replaced Soldado with seven minutes of the match remaining, with the former Real Madrid and Valencia forward leaving the White Hart Lane pitch to a standing ovation. Spurs fans warmed to Soldado during the campaign, despite his poor return in front of goal.

Kane featured in his last Under-21 Premier League match of the season on March 10 as Tottenham beat West Bromwich Albion 5-2. Harry's brace in the match took his tally to eight goals in eight appearances in the division that campaign. He was in the first-team squad for six of Spurs' seven fixtures in all competitions during a busy March and took his place in the starting line-up for the UEFA Europa League round of 16, first leg against Benfica. The Lilywhites exited Europe that season, going down to a 5-3 aggregate defeat to the Portuguese giants, that saw Harry appear as a 71st minute substitute in the second leg.

After Spurs were hammered 4-0 at Anfield on March 30, Sherwood made four changes to the starting line-up for the visit of Sunderland to White Hart Lane the following week. Vlad Chiriches replaced Jan Vertonghen in defence and Paulinho came in for Nabil Bentaleb in midfield. Soldado took his place on the bench, as did Gylfi Sigurdsson while Emmanuel Adebayor and Harry Kane were paired together up front.

The occasion was a proud moment for Kane and his family, as the striker made his first Premier League start in front of a crowd of 34,410 at White Hart Lane. Harry had finally convinced the club's coaching staff he was ready.

"Harry was chomping on the bit to play," recalled First-Team Coach Les Ferdinand. "As a centre-forward myself, I think you get to a level of confidence when you feel 'I'm ready to play, I know what I can do'. Harry had that. We pulled the reigns back on him a bit because we were trying to protect him a bit. But we eventually put him in the side and he just flew from there.

"Tim showed courage putting Harry in the team given (Roberto) Soldado's popularity with the fans. Looking back, with the power of hindsight, I sometimes wonder whether we should have let him off the leash even earlier. In reflection though, that was probably the right time to bring him in. It just happened to be Harry's time."

Ferdinand's fellow First-Team Coach Chris Ramsey felt Kane's performances both in training and matches leading up to the Sunderland game merited his first Premier League start.

"I know sometimes there are circumstances when a player is at a club where a manager likes him and that helps," commented Ramsey. "Whoever you are though, you have to be ready for that opportunity when it comes up. Harry had always shown that he was ready to seize upon any given opportunity. That's exactly what he did when Tim called him into the team."

Lee Cattermole's 17th-minute strike gave relegation-threatened Sunderland the lead in the game. Despite Adebayor's equaliser, there was a disgruntled atmosphere at half-time as a section of the White Hart Lane crowd called for substitute Soldado to be brought on. Spurs made light work of the Black Cats in the second half though and it was Harry who gave them the lead on 59 minutes with a neat finish from a Christian Eriksen cross.

"I remember the goal against Sunderland but it didn't really stand out for me at that time as anything special other than a first league goal for a product of our academy," reflected Daniel Wynne, who was commentating for Spurs TV that night. "The fact Harry went on to score in three successive league games thereafter was impressive and I have clear memories of thinking it would do him a world of good. To be honest though, there was no sign yet of what was to come from him in the years that followed."

Of course, the occasion of his first Premier League goal was far more significant to Kane.

"The goal put us 2-1 up and as soon as I scored it, the emotions just came out," the young striker told Spurs TV. "I thought we played well before Sunderland's goal but we settled down and knew if we played well we'd score goals, that's how it turned out. Christian has a great delivery and whenever he gets on the ball, he's looking to get it into the box. Fortunately, I got in there and scored the goal. I'm delighted.

"It's the best feeling in my career so far. I was buzzing to get my first start in the Premier League for Spurs and to then get my first Premier League goal at White Hart Lane. I've waited patiently and to get that goal is a very proud moment."

A few minutes after scoring his first Premier League goal, Kane was involved in a clash of heads with Wes Brown, leaving both himself and the Sunderland defender requiring treatment. The striker briefly left the field of play to have a bandage fitted around his head. He returned for Spurs' goal-fest in the final 12 minutes of the match that saw Eriksen, Adebayor and Sigurdsson score to give the Lilywhites a comfortable 5-1 victory.

After the game, Kane reflected on an eventful evening and the path to his first Premier League start. "Going on loan (to Leyton Orient) at 17, people did not realise how young I was," he said. "People think I am a bit older but a first Premier League goal for

Tottenham at the age of 20 is not bad. I have been waiting for an opportunity to get a start, so it was great to get the goal and hopefully I can push on and get a few more."

As alluded to by Wynne, Kane scored his second and third Premier League goals for Tottenham in his subsequent appearances. He played his part in a magnificent comeback, as Spurs drew 3-3 at West Bromwich Albion having been 3-0 down. His 70th-minute strike came prior to Eriksen's last-minute leveller. Harry was then on target in a 3-1 win at home to Fulham.

"It's great to be getting some starts recently and three (goals) in three (Premier League starts) is a great (return)," said Kane after the victory over Fulham. "I'm happy to be playing and hopefully we can get results from now until the end of the season. You've got to take your chances at the very top and fortunately I've been able to do that when I've been playing. It has been great but the most important thing today was that we got the result."

Sherwood said of Kane after the match: "He's a top poacher and we always knew he'd score goals. Hopefully he's found his feet in the Premier League."

Harry's run of goals ended in his fourth consecutive Premier League start at Stoke City but a strike from Danny Rose gave Spurs a 1-0 win in the Potteries. He did score on his fifth start, but unfortunately it was at the wrong end as the Lilywhites went down to a 2-0 defeat at West Ham United on May 3.

"I can remember Harry scoring that own goal," said Ramsey. "Did that bother him? No. Tim selected him in the starting line-up again the following week (for a home match with Aston Villa) and that probably gave him that bit of confidence that we believed in him. The fact Tim Sherwood and Les had the confidence to put him into the first-team above certain players like Soldado in the first place was a huge boost for Harry.

"People forget that in the early days when Harry was in the first-team and he might miss a chance or fail to get his shot in quick enough, the fans were singing for Soldado. It took massive bravery from Tim and Les at the time to persevere with him over a player that cost £26m, even knowing that Harry was performing better (than Soldado) at that time. We did the same thing with (Nabil) Bentaleb, putting him in the first-team ahead of Paulinho, who cost the club a large amount of money too."

Tottenham's final match of the 2013-14 season saw them beat Aston Villa 3-0 at White Hart Lane, as they secured a sixth-placed finish in the Premier League and qualification to the Europa League. Kane retained his place in the starting eleven for that match, as goals from Paulinho, Adebayor and an own-goal from Villa's Nathan Baker put the home side three up by half-time. Sherwood's faith in youth continued that afternoon as he brought young Swiss-born, Serbian midfielder Milos Vejkovic on as a second-half substitute for Sandro for just his second Spurs appearance. Fellow academy graduate Benteleb also came on during the match, as did Alex Pritchard, who made his first-team debut when he replaced Gylfi Sigurdsson.

Just two days after Tottenham's victory over Aston Villa, it was announced that Sherwood was to depart White Hart Lane, with club chairman Daniel Levy exercising a break clause in the manager's 18-month contract. Sherwood told Sky Sports News after the announcement: "It is obviously a massive wrench to leave a club of the stature of Tottenham Hotspur, a club very close to my heart."

Given the backing Harry had received from Sherwood throughout his time at Spurs, news of his departure would have been a disappointment for the young striker, especially given his recent run in the first-team. Six days after Sherwood left White Hart Lane, Kane took part in his final match of the season, coming on as a late substitute for Tom Ince in England's Under-21

3-1 away victory in Wales. Kane was replaced minutes later himself by Jake Forster-Caskey, having sustained an ankle injury. The last sighting therefore of Tottenham's young striker, during a campaign in which he had shown so much promise, was of him limping down the tunnel at Swansea City's Liberty Stadium. Thankfully, Harry would be fit and raring to go by the time the Lilywhites visited West Ham United on the opening day of the 2014-15 Premier League season.

On May 28, Kane learnt that his new Tottenham boss was to be Mauricio Pochettino – the former Argentinian international who had nurtured many a young talent in his previous role at Southampton. Luke Shaw, Adam Lallana, Rickie Lambert and Jay Rodriguez all earned their first England caps while Pochettino was in charge at St Mary's. The club achieved their then-joint-highest Premier League finish of eighth while he was there as the Saints racked up impressive victories over the likes of Manchester City, Liverpool and Chelsea.

"There is an abundance of top-class talent at the club and I am looking forward to starting work with the squad," said Pochettino on the back of his appointment as Tottenham Hotspur's new Head Coach.

CHAPTER SEVEN

THE HURRI-KANE ARRIVES

New Tottenham manager Mauricio Pochettino got an early chance to assess his players ahead of the 2014-15 season as the team flew to the United States and Canada for a series of exhibition matches. For Harry Kane, it was the second time he had been to North America with the Lilywhites, having featured in games in Los Angeles, Baltimore and New York in 2012.

"It's a chance to see new cities and we're playing new teams as well," commented Harry as Tottenham arrived ahead of friendly meetings with Seattle Sounders, Toronto FC and Chicago Fire. "They will be fit and ready for us, so it will be a great test and good fitness work for us. That's what it's about."

Kane got to indulge in one of his major sporting passions during the tour – American football. Himself, Etienne Capoue and Gylfi Sigurdsson visited the reigning NFL champions as they took part in a series of sporting challenges with Seattle Seahawks' Doug Baldwin, Steven Hauschka and KJ Wright. Back on the 'soccer' pitch, Kane started in Spurs' opening match of the tour as their 3-3 draw with Seattle Sounders was watched by over 55,000 fans at CenturyLink Field.

Spurs were reunited with a familiar face, as they took on former striker Jermain Defoe and his new team, Toronto FC, on their visit to Canada. Kane came on as a second-half substitute in the 3-2 victory that featured a brace from Erik Lamela and a further goal from Andros Townsend. The North American tour concluded in Illinois where Spurs beat Chicago Fire 2-0 at Toyota Park. Early on, Lewis Holtby pounced on some defensive uncertainty in the Chicago backline, before squaring to Kane on the edge of the six-yard-box. The England Under-21 man made no mistake, finishing from close range. Aaron Lennon added a second with seven minutes of the match remaining.

Pre-season preparations for Kane and Spurs continued in Helsinki in August as the striker opened the scoring in a convincing

6-1 win over Scottish champions Celtic. The Lilywhites' final warm-up match came back in N17, as Emmanual Adebayor and Soldado netted in a 2-1 victory against Schalke 04 that saw Kane appear as a second-half substitute for Lamela.

Days later, it was announced that Harry had agreed a new contact with Spurs, committing his future to the club until 2019. Speaking in the Tottenham programme ahead of the Lilywhites' first Premier League home game of the season against Queens Park Rangers, Kane commented: "I'm very happy to sign this deal and (am) excited for the future. This is one of the proudest days of my football career. It's been fantastic to be at the club that I loved from a kid, growing up watching the team and now to be a part of it. It's all gone so quickly and now to be signing a new deal until 2019, it's a great honour."

Tottenham's summer transfer activity saw them bring the likes of Ben Davies, Michel Vorm, Eric Dier, DeAndre Yedlin, Federico Fazio and Benjamin Stambouli to White Hart Lane – none of which were strikers. The Lilywhites started the season with just three recognised, out-and-out front-men on their books in the shape of Soldado, Adebayor and Kane.

It was Adebayor who was selected to start in a 4-2-3-1 formation at West Ham United on the opening day. In a typically feisty London derby, Kyle Naughton was sent-off for Spurs in the first-half while the Hammers' James Collins got his marching orders in the second. The match was still goalless after 83 minutes when Kane was introduced as a substitute for Adebayor. In the third minute of stoppage time it was Harry who slotted a through-ball into the path of debutant Eric Dier, who rounded Hammers keeper Adrian to net the Lilywhites' winner. Cue scenes of wild celebration in the visitors' end of Upton Park.

Kane's first start that season came as Spurs travelled to Larnaca to face Cypriot side AEL Limassol in the first leg of the UEFA Europa

League play-off. His 80th minute strike completed the visitors' comeback from 1-0 down to win 2-1. He got a goal in the return leg as the Lilywhites booked their place in the group stage with a 5-1 aggregate victory. He also netted in a 1-1 draw with Besitkas before claiming his first hat-trick for Tottenham in a 5-1 victory over Asteras Tripolis at White Hart Lane on October 23, 2014.

It was an entertaining game against Asteras. Kane opened the scoring after 13 minutes before Lamela's famous 'rabona' goal that was subsequently voted the competition's best strike of the season. Lamela's second of the game was followed by two quick-fire strikes from Harry to seal his hat-trick and make it 5-0 to Spurs. Lilywhites goalkeeper Hugo Lloris was sent off late on and with Pochettino having already made three substitutes, it was Kane who volunteered to go in goal. In that moment, the striker must have had a flashback to his trial with Ridgeway Rovers as a six-year-old when he offered to go in between the sticks then too.

While he impressed with his goalkeeping display at Ridgeway all those years ago, Spurs TV commentator Daniel Wynne was right to suggest Kane "shouldn't give up his day job". Moments after putting on the gloves, Harry allowed a tame free-kick from Jeronimo Barrales to squirm under his body to gift Asteras a consolation goal.

"It was a great night until I went in goal," smiled Kane in an interview with ITV4. "In fairness I think I'll leave that to the keepers from now on. It was a great result for us, a great win, and obviously I'm happy to get the hat-trick."

Despite claiming the match ball on the Thursday, Kane returned to the bench that Sunday for Spurs' 2-1 defeat to Newcastle United. Adebayor gave the Lilywhites a bright start but second-half strikes from Sammy Ameobi and Ayoze Perez swung the match in the Magpies' favour. Harry was introduced as a 67th minute substitute for Capoue, briefly partnering Adebayor and then fellow substitute

Soldado up front. He couldn't prevent Tottenham slumping to a disappointing loss though.

In the run-up to Spurs' trip to Aston Villa on November 2, there were growing calls amongst the club's supporters for Kane to command a starting role in the Premier League. "Kane's definitely our most in-form striker, so should get a start tomorrow in my view," wrote one on the independent Tottenham fans' forum *The Fighting Cock* while another added "Argument over. Harry Kane as starting striker for Spurs until further notice. He is ready. It is time."

The striker strengthened his own claim for a starting place by scoring his seventh goal of the season against Brighton & Hove Albion in the League Cup. Harry's strike, before being substituted with five minutes of the match remaining, completed a 2-0 victory for Spurs.

Unusually, given Pochettino's penchant for the 4-2-3-1 formation during that season, two strikers were selected to start for the game at Villa. Alas though, it was Adebayor and Soldado who led the line with Kane back on the bench once again. Spurs' first-half performance was something of a disappointment and Andreas Weimann gave the home side a deserved half-time lead, converting from a Charles N'Zogbia cross.

While Spurs supporters had previously chanted 'he's one of our own' in tribute to Kane, never had it been sung with as much conviction as it was during the second-half of that match at Villa Park. Pochettino answered the fans' calls to bring on the under-21 striker, as Harry replaced Adebayor on 58 minutes. Christian Benteke was sent-off for Aston Villa seven minutes later and with it, a feeling grew amongst the visiting supporters the comeback might be on.

With Kane offering a "significant threat" in his second-half cameo according to the BBC Sport match report, Tottenham grew as an attacking force and equalised with four minutes of normal time remaining through Nacer Chadli. Moments later, the Lilywhites were awarded a free-kick when Townsend was felled by Villa defender Carlos Sanchez. While some of his Spurs teammates expressed an interest in taking the resulting free-kick, it was Kane who picked up the ball and placed it down on the turf with the clear intention of striking it himself.

He did just that, hitting a powerful shot which took a wicked deflection off Villa's Nathan Baker and flew past goalkeeper Brad Guzan. The striker celebrated his late winner by diving along the pitch in front of the travelling Spurs supporters, in a similar style to a certain Jurgen Klinsmann on his Lilywhites debut back in 1994. For added nostalgia, Kane wore Klinsmann's former number 18 shirt throughout the 2014-15 season.

"We can all look on from the stands, or in my case the commentary box, and point to moments that change or define games," reflected Spurs TV commentator Daniel Wynne. "The Aston Villa game was most definitely a turning point in Harry's career. He had missed a penalty earlier in the season at home to Limassol but just a week prior to the Villa game he scored the first of many hat tricks for us in our 5-1 win against Asteras.

"That night was still fresh in everyone's minds when we found ourselves trailing with about eight minutes to play. To put it into context, Villa had lost their previous five League games and we had expected to win. The Spurs fans were all calling for Harry to come off the bench, which he eventually did. The scenes of celebration when the free kick flew in will live long in the memory. He went on to score 21 league goals that season, 31 in all competitions and without doubt, that moment, late at Villa Park was the catalyst for him."

Chris Ramsey recalled seeing the moment when Kane scored against Aston Villa on television. He too saw it as a seminal moment in Harry's career.

"Every player needs those big moments that are a catalyst for change," said Ramsey. "After Harry scored that winner against Aston Villa, he pretty much became one of the first names down on the team sheet overnight. The fans got behind him massively because they related to him. They got behind him too because they loved his commitment."

The goal against Aston Villa had wide reaching implications, not only for Harry but manager Mauricio Pochettino. Having triumphed in just three of his nine opening Premier League matches, the Spurs Head Coach was yet to fully win over the supporters – and possibly the club's board – at that stage of his managerial reign. The Argentinian would later herald the strike as the one that might have saved his job.

"I can find many other goals that were fantastic but, for me, goals are related to emotion, to the period you are living in," Pochettino said in September 2017. "For me, that goal (versus Aston Villa in 2015) was an amazing goal because it meant for us, for everyone, the possibility to stay here today.

"It's true, the team were 14th or 13th (Spurs were actually 11th at that time) and we were a little bit under pressure because the team were playing well, but not winning games and we were a bit under pressure. Always in football, when you don't get good results, the first to be sacked is the manager…

"That is why that goal allowed us to carry on working and try to change the club. We were in the first season at Tottenham and people on day one when I signed the contract said, 'Ok maybe in a few months, we have a new face in front of us!'"

Kane's first start in the Premier League – eleven fixtures into the season – came in a 2-1 defeat to Stoke City. While Soldado reclaimed his place in the team for six of the seven matches thereafter, Kane was soon to make the number nine position his own. Harry scored five goals in five starts from December 17 up to and including

New Years' Day 2015. This included a strike in a 4-0 demolition of Newcastle United in the League Cup and goals in Premier League victories over Burnley and Leicester City.

Kane's 2015 began with a memorable performance against Chelsea. Going into the game, the Blues topped the Premier League table with a three-point lead over Manchester City while the Lilywhites were seventh in the division. Diego Costa gave the West Londoners an early lead but a 20-yard drive from Kane, a Danny Rose strike and a Townsend penalty saw Spurs 3-1 up by half-time. Seven minutes after the break, Kane looked to have put the game to bed as he produced a fine individual goal. Cutting in from the left, the striker evaded the challenges of three Blues defenders before rifling a shot past Thibaut Courtois for his 17th club goal of the season. Cue the now familiar 'he's one of our own' chant from the Tottenham faithful once again.

Eden Hazard gave Chelsea hope with a goal just after the hour mark, but Chadli restored Tottenham's three goal cushion with 12 minutes remaining. A late header from John Terry wasn't enough to dampen the mood at White Hart Lane as the home side ran out 5-3 winners.

"Beating Chelsea is always memorable but putting five past them, at home, on New Year's Day with four goals coming from players that progressed through our youth set up (Kane, Townsend and Danny Rose) will always be special," reflected Wynne. "We battered them that day and for me it was a coming of age for Harry Kane. To destroy the Chelsea defence in the way he did that day told me that we had a special player on our hands. He ran them ragged and his goals stood out. What a player, what a game."

Whereas Kane had previously been selected for cup games and left out of Premier League matches by Pochettino, it was now the other way around. He was on the bench for the Lilywhites' third round tie and replay with Burnley and the fourth round defeat to Leicester City. Harry took his place in the starting eleven for league fixtures against Crystal Palace and West Bromwich Albion though, that saw him net three times. He also started both legs of the Lilywhites' League Cup semi-final clash with Sheffield United.

On January 21, Pochettino's team travelled to a snowy Bramall Lane for the second leg of the League Cup semi-final, which they led 1-0 from the first meeting. Christian Eriksen give the visitors – chasing their first cup final appearance since 2009 – the lead after 28 minutes. However, a late fightback saw the hosts draw level on aggregate as Che Adams netted in both the 77th and 79th minute.

Over the years, Tottenham supporters have become all too familiar with a certain tag known as 'Spursy', defined by *Urban Dictionary* as a "consistent and inevitable failure to live up to expectations". Rocked by Adams' late goals, the 5,000-strong away following might have feared another 'Spursy' moment against lower league opposition. But the Lilywhites have shown throughout Pochettino's reign that the team are now made of sterner stuff. Proof of that came with Eriksen's second strike of the game two minutes from time that staved off any chance of an upset. Spurs' 3-2 aggregate victory secured a Wembley showdown with Chelsea on March 1 in the League Cup Final.

Four players who progressed through Tottenham's academy – Kane, Townsend, Rose and Ryan Mason – featured in the semi-final matches against the Blades, emphasising the faith Pochettino has had in Spurs' youngsters throughout his time with the north London club.

"Mauricio has shown massive confidence in Harry and other younger players during his time at Tottenham," commented former Spurs Assistant Academy Manager Ramsey. "Let's face it, when he (Pochettino) first arrived at Spurs, the temptation must have been to raise a war chest for new signings by selling youngsters like Harry,

Ryan Mason, Andros Townsend, Nabil Bentaleb etc. He could have just thought 'they're not quite ready yet'. Instead, he put his faith in them, gave them their chance and he was rewarded. I think Harry's development – and numerous other players – has been topped off by him working with Pochettino. He's done a magnificent job with Harry."

Spurs faced five matches in February 2015 prior to their League Cup Final with Chelsea. The first of those fixtures was at home to rivals Arsenal on the seventh of the month. For Kane, the game represented the opportunity to play in the north London derby at senior level and to take on the club that released him at the age of eight for the first time.

"I remember the first time we played against Arsenal... and even back then, I had a chip on my shoulder," Kane told *The Players' Tribune*. "It might sound ridiculous — I was only eight when they let me go — but every time we played them, I thought, 'alright, we'll see who's right and who's wrong'. Looking back on it (being released by Arsenal as a youngster) now, it was probably the best thing that ever happened to me, because it gave me a drive that wasn't there before."

At that time, Tottenham hadn't finished above their north London rivals in the last 18 Premier League seasons. Under Pochettino's management though, there was a general feeling that Spurs were closing the gap on the Gunners. Indeed, there were just two points separating the teams at kick-off that afternoon, with the Lilywhites knowing they could leap-frog Arsene Wenger's side with a victory.

Mesut Ozil's tenth minute strike gave the visitors a 1-0 half-time lead. Buoyed by the energy from the White Hart Lane crowd, Spurs looked capable of an equaliser though. The moment duly arrived nine minutes in to the second period when Kane tapped in from close range after Gunners goalkeeper David Ospina palmed

Mousa Dembele's header from a corner into his path. With just a few minutes of the match remaining, Nabil Bentaleb swung a fine, left-footed cross into the Arsenal penalty area. Standing just outside the six-yard box, Kane's flighted header past Ospina saw him become Tottenham's match winner in his first North London derby.

"He was the hero before, now he's the messiah," screamed BT Sport commentator Darren Fletcher as Kane's header hit the back of the net, while Spurs supporter Daniel Wynne was in raptures.

"There were some goals that literally left the gantry at White Hart Lane rocking and that was one of them," reflected Wynne on Kane's winner. "The commentary box used to hang from the East Stand roof and when all four sides of the ground were up, singing, cheering, clapping, stamping their feet etc, it would literally sway. When Arsenal visited the Lane, the atmosphere was always special and our 2-1 win in February 2015 was no different. We conceded first but by the time the day was done, normal service had been resumed thanks to a brace from the hottest property in the Premier League.

"I remember the second goal, a header which gave David Ospina no chance in the Arsenal goal. It was another late strike and they couldn't respond. When it went in, I remember saying in commentary that 'White Hart Lane is rocking' as from where I was perched, it really was. He loves scoring against Arsenal and has since made quite a habit of doing so. Long may that continue!"

Kane himself said it was a "dream come true" to score twice on his north London derby debut;

"It was incredible, the fans were incredible and the atmosphere was lightning. They made it better for us, we played our football, and that feeling is one I won't forget probably for the rest of my career. I enjoy my football; play with a smile on your face, do the best you can and work as hard as you can for the team.

"I'm enjoying it, I just want to be out on that pitch and playing with my mates, playing with the people that I'm around every day. I don't think I can put it into words. Obviously, my first north London derby, to win the way we did and dig deep, it's incredible. I probably won't sleep tonight."

Then-England manager Roy Hodgson was in the stands that afternoon and subsequently named Harry in the senior squad for the first time for upcoming matches with Lithuania and Italy. Prior to joining up with the Three Lions camp, Kane suffered the disappointment of defeat in his first cup final appearance as Spurs lost 2-0 to Chelsea. Despite that set-back, the striker's red-hot goal-scoring form continued throughout the month as he got two goals at Queens Park Rangers and his first Premier League hat-trick in a 4-3 win over Leicester City.

On March 27, Kane replaced Wayne Rooney as a 72nd minute substitute at Wembley to make his senior England debut against Lithuania in a UEFA Euro 2016 qualifier. It couldn't have gone better. The Three Lions were leading 3-0 when he was introduced to the game and within 79 seconds, he made it four with a far-post header. "I ran on the pitch and the cheer I got at Wembley was amazing, it gave me goosebumps," Kane told the Football Association's official website. "Then a minute or so later, I scored and the emotion was just amazing. Maybe you think moments like that will never happen for you, but these opportunities have come my way and thankfully I have been able to take them."

Harry had touched the ball just three times prior to his first senior international goal. "50 more touches and Harry Kane will beat Sir Bobby Charlton's (then) goal scoring record (for England)," joked Gary Lineker as the striker followed in the footsteps of the likes of Sir Stanley Matthews, Sir Tom Finney, Sir Bobby Charlton, Jimmy Greaves and Alan Shearer by scoring on his England debut.

Harry, who went on to start in England's friendly in Italy a few days later, reflected on his goal scoring debut for the Three Lions: "I'm just proud. A dream come true. It's a special night and definitely one I won't forget. It's what you dream of as a kid, it's a bit of a daze and enjoying every minute of it."

On his return from England duties, Kane started the remaining eight matches of Tottenham's season, scoring in away wins at Newcastle United and Everton on the final day of the campaign. The Lilywhites improved on their performance of the previous season by finishing fifth in the Premier League, once again booking a place in the UEFA Europa League. Alas, they fell short in their attempts to finish higher in the table than north London rivals Arsenal though, who came third with an 11-point advantage over Spurs.

Despite not leap-frogging the Gunners, the 2014-15 season was an undoubted success story for Tottenham. And what a campaign it had been for Kane, who scored 21 goals in the league and struck 31 times overall for the Lilywhites as he finished up as the club's top scorer. Only Sergio Aguero, with 26 strikes, bettered Harry's Premier League tally while he manged one more goal than Chelsea's title-winning forward Diego Costa and five more than Arsenal's Alexis Sanchez.

Kane was rewarded for his form with the PFA Young Player of the Year award and also took his place in the PFA Premier League Team of the Year. He scooped back-to-back Premier League Player of the Month awards in January and February 2015 and was both One Hotspur Members' Player of the Season and One Hotspur Junior Members' Player of the Season. Reflecting on his performances that campaign in the club's official annual meanwhile, Kane commented;

"Crazy, incredible and one I'll never forget. I think it was a good season, our form was a little up and down but we've had young players coming through and we've built a platform which we have to build on."

Harry was the star-turn for Spurs' end of season matches in Malaysia and Australia, emphasised by the fact the club had to send a minibus to collect himself, Tom Carroll and Ryan Mason from the Westfield shopping centre in Sydney when they were mobbed by fans. Not that Kane was too concerned by the attention.

"I don't mind it," he said. "Obviously it's just the start for me. Maybe, in the years to come, I'll get a bit grumpy, but it's fine. I've always been happy to talk to fans. You don't know how far they've travelled just to meet you. So, if you don't sign something, or don't talk to them, it could be heart-breaking for them. I was a fan once and I'd always want someone I've admired to be a nice guy. That's what I try and be. I don't think that will ever change. I think I'll always sign stuff for fans and take pictures because I know how much it means."

Despite having made his England senior debut during the season, Kane travelled with the under-21s to the UEFA European Under-21 Championships in the Czech Republic in June. Much was expected from Gareth Southgate's young team – as it had been the case when England went to Turkey for the UEFA European Under-19 Championships in 2012. Unfortunately, there was to be more disappointment in Eastern Europe, as Southgate's men were beaten by Portugal and Italy and finished bottom of Group B. Kane played the full 90 minutes in all three group games, with his appearance in the 3-1 defeat on June 24, 2015 being his last for the Under-21s. Kane scored eight times in 14 appearances at that level.

While England's early exit from the competition would have soured Kane's summer, greater international targets lay ahead as he looked to help the senior side achieve qualification for UEFA Euro 2016 and secure himself a place in Roy Hodgson's tournament squad in the process.

CHAPTER EIGHT

ONE SEASON WONDER

Tottenham's sale of striker Roberto Soldado to Villarreal and subsequent release of forward Emmanual Adebayor during the summer of 2015 spoke volumes for the confidence manager Mauricio Pochettino had in Harry Kane going into the new season. Spurs' acquisitions that window included defenders Kevin Wimmer, Toby Alderweireld and Kieran Trippier. After Spurs' 1-0 defeat at Manchester United on the opening day of the season, two additional signings were made in the shape of Clinton N'Jie and Heung-Min Son. Both were attack-minded players but not out-and-out 'number nines' in the Kane mould.

Tottenham provided the opposition for the MLS All-Star game on July 29 in which Kane scored in the 2-1 defeat. After leaving the States, Pochettino's men travelled on to Germany for the four-team Audi Cup, featuring European heavyweights AC Milan, Bayern Munich and Real Madrid.

The tournament served to highlight the ability of another Tottenham youngster – Dele Alli – who was signed from MK Dons in January 2015 but instantly loaned back to his former club. Despite losing 2-0 to Real Madrid in the opening match, the abiding image for Spurs supporters was of Alli nutmegging their former midfielder Luka Modric during an impressive display. Goals from Nacer Chadli and Tom Carroll saw Spurs finish third at the tournament with a 2-0 victory over AC Milan while hosts Bayern Munich lifted the trophy.

After the 1-0 defeat to Manchester United on the opening day of the campaign, Spurs' early season form was solid rather than spectacular. They drew three of their four Premier League fixtures, which included a 2-2 tie at Leicester City – a result that would become more significant as the season went on. The Lilywhites beat Qarabag 3-1 in the UEFA Europa League in September in between victories over Sunderland and Crystal Palace while Spurs were knocked out of the League Cup by rivals Arsenal.

Kane failed to score for Tottenham in eight appearances at the start of the campaign but he did find the back of the net for England during that period. He was on target in a 6-0 win in San Marino and in a 2-0 triumph over Switzerland at Wembley as Roy Hodgson's team sealed qualification for UEFA Euro 2016. Despite his goals for the Three Lions, Harry's dry spell at club level led to accusations from rival fans and sections of the media that he was 'just a one-season wonder'. Not that anyone at White Hart Lane was concerned.

"He has just been a bit unlucky," Jan Vertonghen told a press conference." He scored for England and in the training sessions he has been doing very well, so the goals will come. He's not a guy who will just have one good season and then you never see him again. He has the qualities to perform and the goals will come eventually."

The goals did indeed arrive for Spurs, with Kane's first strike of the club campaign coming on September 26 – a day when Tottenham hammered pre-season title favourites Manchester City 4-1. Kevin de Bruyne opened the scoring for the visitors before Eric Dier equalised on the stroke of half-time. After the break, Toby Alderweireld headed Spurs in front before the moment the White Hart Lane faithful had been waiting for. Kane finished from close range after Christian Eriksen had hit the woodwork with a free-kick – ending his 748-minute run without a competitive goal for the Lilywhites.

"It was always a case of when, not if with H," reflected Richard 'Crackers' Cracknell – who hosts the Spurs podcast *Ohh When The Spurs* (follow @ohhwhenthespurs on Twitter) – on Kane's goal against City. "Harry has always had that 'X factor'. I never have and never will place any value on the opinion of other teams' fans on our players. For me, silly comments mean that you're doing something right."

Erik Lamela rounded off a memorable afternoon with his side's fourth goal eleven minutes from time. The result moved Spurs into fifth position in the league and to within four points of leaders Manchester United. After the game, Kane said he had never doubted himself during his lean spell.

"There's been a lot of talk but I'm a confident man and have faith in my ability," Kane told BT Sport. "I'm delighted. It was a very good victory against a team who were top of the table."

Kane reported for international duty shortly after, starting the Three Lions' final European qualifying victories over Estonia at Wembley and away to Lithuania. Later in the month, the Lilywhites triumphed 5-1 in their first-ever Premier League visit to AFC Bournemouth. Kane got a hat-trick that afternoon at the start of an incredible scoring run for the striker, who bagged nine goals in six consecutive matches for Spurs.

He was on target in a 3-1 Premier League win over Aston Villa and a 2-1 triumph against Anderlecht in the Europa League at the start of November. His red-hot form continued on his first visit to the Emirates Stadium with Tottenham. The Gunners were still smarting from their 5-1 defeat to Bayern Munich and Spurs inflicted more misery on their rivals when Kane broke free after 32 minutes and coolly slotted past Petr Cech.

"The display away at Arsenal was a wonderful performance from Kane," recalled Mike Leigh, who has been the presenter of the *Spurs Show* (www.spursshow.net) podcast since 2007. "He took his goal brilliantly and his all-round display gave a glimpse of what was to come. Not only was he looking the real deal, you kind of sensed how much the club and the fans meant to him with his displays against our rivals."

The only disappointment after an excellent display at the Emirates was that Spurs couldn't hold out for all three points.

Substitute Kieran Gibbs capped an improved second-half showing from Arsenal to grab an equaliser 13 minutes from time. Gibbs and Kane would meet up shortly after the north London derby, having been named in the squad for England's friendlies with Spain and France in mid-November. Spurs team-mates Kyle Walker and Dele Alli were also included in the 23-man group, as was Eric Dier, who was selected for the senior squad for the first time.

Kane started both matches – a 2-0 loss to Spain in Alicante and a 2-0 win over France at Wembley. While he didn't score on international duty, the striker picked up where he had left off with Tottenham with a brace against West Ham United in a 4-1 win. That was followed by the only goal against Qarabag which secured the north Londoners' progress to the knockout phase of the Europa League. Reigning champions Chelsea finally managed to stop the striker in his tracks, securing a goalless draw at White Hart Lane at the end of the month.

After 14 rounds of the Premier League season, Manchester City led the table – level on 29 points with surprise package, Leicester City. The Foxes had been 5000-1 outsiders for the title at the start of the campaign. Many expected their charge to falter in December 2015 but three straight victories kept their unlikely dream alive. A month earlier, former Leicester striker Gary Lineker vowed to present *Match of the Day* in his pants if his home town club went on to be crowned champions.

Just four points behind, some people were even beginning to mention Spurs' name in the title shake-up too. But after a stalemate with Chelsea, a 1-1 draw at West Bromwich Albion and a 2-1 home defeat to Newcastle United, expectations of a first title triumph since 1961 weren't exactly going through the roof at White Hart Lane. The draw for Euro 2016 on December 12 offered Kane a brief distraction from club affairs as he discovered England had been paired with Slovakia, Russia and teammate Ben Davies' Wales at the tournament.

After a few set-backs, the Christmas fixtures rekindled hope of a very happy new year for Tottenham Hotspur, with the club racking up three straight wins over Southampton, Norwich City and Watford. Kane scored against the Saints and twice against the Canaries. Spurs' 2-1 victory at Vicarage Road on December 28 put Pochettino's team third in the Premier League – just four points behind new title leaders Arsenal.

The Lilywhites had been drawn to face Leicester City in the third round of the FA Cup in January 2016, but the fixture date every supporter had ringed in their diary was the Premier League clash between the two clubs that month. A win for Tottenham would have moved them just one point behind Claudio Ranieri's team and three behind leaders Arsenal, depending on how the Gunners got on at Liverpool that same night.

Spurs boasted 62% possession against Leicester and managed 21 shots to the Foxes' ten. On 62 minutes, the home side looked like making their advantage pay when Erik Lamela played Kane through on Kasper Schmeichel's goal. The England striker got a good connection with the ball, but the on-rushing keeper's touch was enough to see it bounce off the turf and onto the crossbar. With seven minutes remaining, Robert Huth headed in from a Leicester corner to confirm a 1-0 away victory and a pivotal result in both teams' season.

Spurs bounced back from the disappointment with a 4-1 thrashing of Sunderland in N17, which again featured a Kane goal. They also exacted a small amount of revenge on the Foxes, winning 2-0 at the King Power Stadium in the FA Cup third round replay. Kane had come off the bench to score in the original cup tie that finished in a 2-2 draw.

One of Tottenham's most scintillating performances of the season came at Norwich City in the first week of February. Dele Alli put Spurs one up after just a few minutes at Carrow Road and a Kane penalty made it two before half-time. Unfortunately Alli, who had been in imperious form in the first 45 minutes, had to go off at the break as he was feeling unwell. The Lilywhites continued their dominance in the second period as they managed 17 attempts during the game and sealed a 3-0 win with a second goal from Kane.

"He (Kane) was absolutely on fire that night," said Spurs fan Crackers. "There was nothing that Norwich could do that day to stop him. To be fair, Dele was also brilliant before he went off ill."

Momentum continued to build for the Lilywhites as their 1-0 victory over Watford on February 6 took them up to second in the table. They were five points behind leaders Leicester City, who recorded an impressive 3-1 win at Manchester City that same day. By this point, the Premier League title race looked like a four-club affair involving the Foxes, Spurs, City and Arsenal.

Tottenham were a point ahead of third-placed Manchester City prior to a visit to the Etihad Stadium on Valentine's Day. A key moment in the game occurred on 52 minutes when City's Raheem Sterling was adjudged – perhaps harshly – to have handled the ball in his own penalty area. Kane swept home the subsequent spot kick for his 15th goal in his last 17 Premier League appearances.

Substitute Kelechi Iheanacho equalised for the home side with 16 minutes remaining to set-up a grandstand finish. Spurs rode their luck at times, as the home side managed 19 attempts to the Lilywhites' six. However, most neutral observers would have thought the visitors deserving of Christian Eriksen's winner that came their way seven minutes from time. The 2-1 win closed the gap on leaders Leicester to just two points. The White Hart Lane faithful were now daring to dream about what might be possible for their team.

Harry celebrates his goal against Tunisia in England's 2018 World Cup opener

The famous shot of Harry and his now fiancée Katie meeting David Beckham in 2005

Harry makes his Tottenham debut against Hearts in August 2011

On loan at Leyton Orient   On loan at Leicester City

On loan at Millwall

Kane's first Tottenham goal, scored against Shamrock Rovers in December 2011

Spurs coaching team Les Ferdinand and Chris Ramsey trained Kane at every level

Celebrating a goal in his first Premier League start

Celebrating a goal against Arsenal in 2015

Harry bags another goal against Arsenal in 2015

Harry scores against Lithuania in his England debut in March 2015

Scoring for Spurs against Manchester United in the last game
at White Hart Lane in May 2016

Harry Kane and Hugo Lloris visit the new Tottenham Hotspur Stadium site

Cristiano Ronaldo and Harry Kane meet at
a Champions League group game in 2017

Sporting the captain's armband at the 2018 World Cup

Harry celebrating with his family

Proposing to his fiancée Katie Goodland in the Bahamas

Harry has been active doing charity work with Noah's Ark Children's Hospice

Work continues on Tottenham Hotspur's new stadium

Harry celebrates after scoring a penalty during the Russia 2018
World Cup Group G match between England and Panama

"In the minds of traditional and pessimist Spurs fans, the City away game would be the one where we would come unstuck but the win truly showed how far we had come as a team," commented Spurs fan Mike Leigh. "No one held any fear to us anymore and the memory of previous capitulations there were certainly banished. Here was a young side who loved playing in the Lilywhite shirt with a young manager urging them on."

Fellow Spurs fan and podcaster Crackers agreed with Leigh's glowing sentiments. "After that win I made the fatal mistake of really allowing myself to dream it (the Premier League title) was on," he said. "It was just beginning to feel so different for Spurs with a will to win and get over the line I hadn't seen in a long while."

Prior to another important league match with Swansea City the club faced three back-to-back cup matches. A fifth round FA Cup exit at the hands of Crystal Palace was sandwiched in between progress in the Europa League as Spurs beat Fiorentina 4-2 on aggregate. Tottenham trailed at half-time in their league meeting with Swansea but Nacer Chadli equalised and Danny Rose's 77th minute strike gave Pochettino's side a 2-1 win. Leicester's draw at home to West Bromwich Albion two days later meant Spurs travelled to West Ham United on March 2 with the chance to top the Premier League on goal difference with a win. Alas, it wasn't to be. Kane was unable to find the back of the net for his third game in a row and his team went down to a 1-0 defeat on a painful night for Tottenham players and fans alike.

"The loss at West Ham was a real double blow," said Crackers. "The fixture at that stage was a crucial must win but we lost. The fact it was to them (West Ham) made it even worse."

Spurs had another chance to go top of the league – albeit just for a few hours potentially – as they hosted Arsenal on March 5 in a 12:45pm kick-off while leaders Leicester got underway at Watford at 3pm. A massive game for the Lilywhites, the derby was also hugely significant for the Gunners – who were three points behind their north London rivals at the start of play and harboured title ambitions of their own.

Arsenal led at half-time through an Aaron Ramsey goal but Spurs equalised on the hour mark through Toby Alderweireld. Two minutes later Kane – sporting a face mask having broken his nose against Crystal Palace in the FA Cup – curled a magnificent shot past David Ospina from a tight angle. The mask instantly came off as Harry celebrated what looked like being a memorable north London derby winner.

"It's still my favourite Kane goal in a Spurs shirt," commented Leigh. "The hustle from Dele to win the ball back was fantastic as was Kane's audacity to try that kind of shot from the angle he was at. His run towards the Shelf after scoring and the slide celebration will always live with me."

Sadly, for the majority of the 35,762 fans inside White Hart Lane, Kane's cracker wasn't to bring Spurs all three points as Alexis Sanchez equalised with 14 minutes to go. With Leicester winning 1–0 at Vicarage Road that afternoon, the draw did neither Tottenham or Arsenal many favours in terms of their title ambitions.

While Spurs were knocked out of the Europa League by Borussia Dortmund in March 2016, Kane's goals helped keep the Lilywhites on Leicester's coattails at the top of the Premier League. The striker got braces in wins over Aston Villa and AFC Bournemouth, prior to reporting for international duty. He featured in an impressive comeback from England – who won 3-2 against Germany in Berlin having been 2-0 down – scoring the first of the Three Lions' goals. He then came on as a substitute in a 2–1 defeat to the Netherlands at Wembley a few days later.

After the internationals, Kane was on the scoresheet in Tottenham's 1–1 draw at Liverpool while he started in their 3-0 victory over Manchester United. Leicester's 2–2 draw at home to West Ham on April 17 gave Spurs the chance to close the gap at the top of the division to five points with a win at Stoke City. Pochettino's men did just that with Harry managing yet another brace in a 4-0 triumph. After the game, the striker posted an image of a pride of lions on his Instagram account, seemingly making a statement that the Lilywhites were hunting down the Foxes.

Leicester responded with a 4-0 win over Swansea City before Spurs' home match with West Bromwich Albion. Tottenham went ahead through a Craig Dawson own goal but their title hopes were dashed in the second-half when the same player scored at the right end. The 1–1 draw put Leicester within one win of the Premier League crown. Manager Mauricio Pochettino insisted the Lilywhites "still need to believe" after the match that saw his side hit the woodwork three times. Realistically though, the last chance of the north London side winning the league that season had gone.

The Foxes' 1–1 draw at Manchester United on May 1 at least delayed the seemingly inevitable. And when Kane and Heung-Min Son put Spurs two up at Chelsea the following night, the title race looked like it would continue into the penultimate round of Premier League fixtures. The Lilywhites needed a win at Chelsea for that scenario to become a reality. Tottenham supporters were nervy when Gary Cahill pulled a goal back for the Blues in the second-half before the ultimate dagger blow. With seven minutes of the match remaining Eden Hazard – a one-time reported transfer target for Tottenham – curled an unstoppable shot into the roof of Hugo Lloris' net to draw Chelsea level. A bad-tempered match simmered over late on as no less than 12 yellow cards were shown that evening – nine to Spurs players. Harry's own booking came for a foul on Willian in the last minute of stoppage time.

"I don't think a Spurs game has ever stirred such emotions," said Crackers of the 2–2 draw. "Chelsea went toe-to-toe with us in a football match that night and couldn't live with us. I was so proud of the mature performance. But then Chelsea took us down a different avenue and we got absolutely schooled. They went to war with us and foolishly we obliged. That match showed that we had a great football ability but still a naivety in game management. As frustrating as it was to see us get suckered in to the scrap, I was also hugely proud to see a Spurs team that would go to war for each other. I think we learnt a hell of a lot that night that has helped us to grow for subsequent seasons."

The final whistle after the game later dubbed the 'Battle of Stamford Bridge' meant Leicester City were crowned as Premier League title-winners for the first time in their history. Images of Jamie Vardy 'having a party' were beamed across the world, while the city that is the resting place of King Edward III celebrated the achievements of their newly-crowned footballing royalty. Kane's England teammate Vardy also found the time to post an image from the Disney film, *The Lion King*, on his Twitter account, showing lion Mufasa falling to his death among a stampede of wildebeest – an obvious riposte to Harry's Instagram post a few weeks earlier.

After the title dream died, Spurs' season fizzled out with a 2–1 home defeat to Southampton followed by a 5–1 capitulation at the hands of relegated Newcastle United. To make matters worse, Arsenal pipped them to second place in the Premier League table, finishing a point above Mauricio Pochettino's team. Despite the pain of those final weeks, it had still been a great campaign for Tottenham, who secured their first qualification for the UEFA Champions League since 2010–11.

In just his second full season in the Spurs first-team, the campaign was a massive success for Kane too. He won his first Premier League Golden Boot with 25 goals in 38 matches while he netted 28 times in 50 club appearances overall. He was also named in the PFA Premier League Team of the Year for a second successive season.

Kane was included in Roy Hodgson's preliminary squad of 26 players for Euro 2016 on May 16 – a squad that was whittled down to 23 a few weeks later, as Andros Townsend, Danny Drinkwater and Fabien Delph missed out on final selection. Ahead of the striker's first appearance at a major international tournament, Harry scored in a 2–1 friendly victory against Turkey and also featured in 1–0 warm-up triumph over Portugal.

The Tottenham frontman started in England's opening two Group B matches at the tournament as a 1–1 draw with Russia and a 2–1 win over Wales put the Three Lions on the brink of automatic qualification for the knockout phase. Kane – who was substituted at half-time against Wales – came off the bench in the goalless draw with Slovakia in the final group game in Saint-Etienne. While the result guaranteed the Three Lions' progression to the next round as group runners-up to Wales, boos could be heard from sections of their supporters, unhappy with their team's displays in France so far.

Kane was back in England's starting eleven for the round of 16 match against Iceland on June 27. Wayne Rooney's penalty put the Three Lions one-up after just four minutes but goals from Ragnar Sigurdsson and Kolbeinn Sigthorsson turned the match on its head and put the pre-tournament 150/1 shots Iceland – with a country population of just over 330,000 – 2–1 up by half-time.

BBC Sport's Phil McNulty used the words "nervous", "unsettled" and "poor" to describe individual performances from England players that evening. And after the final whistle sounded in Nice – confirming the Three Lions' 2–1 defeat – he went as far as to describe the result as the nation's "worst humiliation since they were knocked out of the 1950 World Cup by USA in Brazil." Alan

Shearer added to the criticism, calling the display from Hodgson's side "hopeless", "tactically inept" and the "worst performance I've ever seen from an England team."

"It looked to me like Roy (Hodgson) was making it up as he was going along," continued Shearer during the BBC's post-match coverage. "How can he pick Arsenal midfielder Jack Wilshere? We had players in the squad who didn't deserve to be there. Manchester City's winger Raheem Sterling hasn't performed. We can go on and on. Then there was Tottenham striker Harry Kane on corners… the list is endless."

Hodgson's instruction for Kane to take corners, rather than get in the box for those set-pieces, was a major topic of conversation for England fans and the media alike. At one point in a match against Wales, it is understood that Wayne Rooney relieved Harry of corner taking duties without the manager's permission. After England's 1–0 victory over Slovakia in September 2016, Kane addressed the tactical hot potato with journalists.

"I will probably never take another corner," smiled Kane. "It's obviously a laugh and a joke now. We had a bit of a laugh and a joke with the manager about it, but it's something that happened. I am happy to be in the box and hopefully I will get a goal for it. It has become a bit of a thing now on social media.

"You have just got to laugh with it. Of course, it was a disappointing moment in the summer but it's football. It's what makes and breaks you as a player. It's what grows you up as a player and that is what I have got to use to help me."

While Kane was to bounce back from the disappointment of Euro 2016, the tournament was to be the breaking point for England manager Roy Hodgson who resigned moments after the defeat to Iceland. "I'm sorry it will have to end this way but these things happen," said Hodgson in a post-match press conference.

CHAPTER NINE

FAREWELL TO THE LANE

On April 28, 2017, Tottenham Hotspur Football Club announced their last-ever match at White Hart Lane was to be their final home game of the campaign against Manchester United. As the construction of the club's new stadium – being built just a few hundred yards north of the current ground – continued, it had been obvious for many months beforehand that it was going to be the Lane's swansong season.

With 118 years of history at the old ground, there was a nostalgic feel in N17 from the first home match of the season. Prior to the visit of Crystal Palace on August 20, 2016 a section of the north-east corner of the stadium had been removed to accommodate the new build. As a result, the structure of the East Stand, which dates back to 1934, became visible. For a number of home games thereafter – until a stairwell for the new stadium eventually blocked the view – supporters had an active glimpse into Tottenham Hotspur's past. In the present meanwhile, a late goal from new signing Victor Wanyama gave Spurs a 1-0 win over the Eagles that day.

At the start of the 2016-17 season, even the usually future-focused Harry Kane was involved in a spot of reflection on the events of the previous campaign and told Spurs TV;
"Looking back now, it (2015-16) was a great season for us. We would have taken that at the start of last year. It's just a shame the way things ended, because we played better than that (the last few games) throughout the season."

Before the new season kicked off, Tottenham travelled to Australia to compete in the International Champions Cup. After his exertions at Euro 2016, Kane was one of several Spurs players, including Hugo Lloris, Eric Dier, Dele Alli, Kyle Walker, Toby Alderweireld, Jan Vertonghen and Ben Davies, to stay in the UK and rest while their teammates departed for Melbourne. The striker's only outing during pre-season saw him score twice in the Lilywhites' 6-1 triumph over Inter Milan in Oslo.

In addition to Wanyama, the club's other signings during the 2016 summer transfer window included Georges-Kevin N'Koudou and Moussa Sissoko, as well as Dutch international striker Vincent Janssen. The signing from AZ Alkmaar was expected to provide cover, complement and also to compete with Kane for a starting role in Mauricio Pochettino's frontline.

The Lilywhites drew 1-1 at Everton on the opening weekend of the Premier League season, before picking up their first three points with the aforementioned victory over Crystal Palace. A 1-1 draw with Liverpool at the end of August moved Spurs up to sixth place in the early standings with five points from a possible nine.

Newly appointed England boss Sam Allardyce selected Kane in his first Three Lions squad for their opening 2018 FIFA World Cup qualifier in Slovakia in what proved to be 'Big Sam's' one and only match in charge of the national team. Harry started, as Adam Lallana's stoppage time goal secured a 1-0 away win for England. When Allardyce departed his new position a few weeks later, he could at least boast a 100% record as Three Lions boss.

The Slovakia fixture saw Kane extend his run without a goal for club and country to nine consecutive matches. Quizzed on the supposed 'goal drought' by the media after the game, Kane wasn't feeling the need to panic, pointing to the fact he didn't score for Spurs during the 2015-16 season until the end of September yet still ended with 32 goals for his club during the campaign.

"As a striker I want to get goals, it doesn't matter who I am playing," said Kane. "I didn't score (against Slovakia) but I felt we all put in a good shift for the team and worked hard for each other. Hopefully if I am picked for the next game or the next squad hopefully I can get a few goals and see what happens.

"What happened last season has given me confidence. Unfortunately, there was a lot of talk last year and I managed to prove a lot of people wrong so people will talk this year as well. It's part of football. I am confident in my ability. I know that if I continue doing what I am doing the goals will come, that is all I can do. I didn't score in my first seven or eight games last season and then to go on and win the Golden Boot proves that it was just a matter of time."

Kane's first competitive club goal duly arrived on his first match back after international duty. His 70th minute strike at Stoke City completed a 4-0 victory as Spurs won by the same score line they had done on their last visit to the bet365 Stadium.

With a reduced capacity at White Hart Lane in the ground's final season, Tottenham Hotspur decided to switch the venue of their UEFA Champions League home games to Wembley. A club-record crowd – indeed the largest ever home attendance for an English club – of 85,011 were at the national stadium for Spurs' first Group E fixture against AS Monaco. The Lilywhites had thrashed them 4-1 in the UEFA Europa League during the previous season but found Leonardo Jardim's side a far more difficult prospect nearly 12 months on.

By the 31st minute, Spurs were 2-0 down. Toby Alderweireld's header pulled a goal back for the Lilywhites just before half-time but they were unable to complete a second-half comeback as the Ligue 1 side held on for a 2-1 away victory. It was a disappointing start to life in Europe's premier club competition for Kane, who missed a decent chance to equalise late on.

Back in the Premier League, Tottenham extended their unbeaten start to the season to five matches with a hard-fought victory over Sunderland. It wasn't until Spurs' 22nd shot and the 59th minute of the game that they finally opened the scoring, with Kane beating Black Cats' goalkeeper Jordan Pickford from close-range. While there was delight at the 1-0 win, there was concern at the sight of Harry being carried off on a stretcher with a nasty looking ankle injury. He subsequently missed the next ten Spurs fixtures as well as England's World Cup qualifiers with Malta and Slovenia.

In the days leading up to the first north London derby of the season, manager Mauricio Pochettino gave Spurs fans the news they had been longing for. "Harry will be in the squad (for the match against Arsenal on November 6)," Pochettino said. "I can confirm he will be available to be selected. I need to decide whether to start him or put him on the bench. I am happy after Thursday. He had a very good training session. He is fit. Always, Harry is important. In the last two seasons, he has been very important for us – he was the top scorer in the Premier League. It's very good news. It's good that he will be back."

Pochettino put Kane straight back in to Tottenham's starting line-up for the match at the Emirates Stadium. Arsenal had the chance to go top of the table with a win that afternoon and seemed on track to do just that when the unfortunate Kevin Wimmer put through his own net. After Laurent Koscielny tangled with Mousa Dembele in the Arsenal penalty area in the second half, there was only one candidate to take the resulting spot kick. Kane stepped up and confidently levelled, showing no signs of rustiness after his seven-week spell on the side lines. The visitors could have even left N7 with all three points but for a fine save by Gunners keeper Petr Cech from a Christian Eriksen free-kick.

New England manager Gareth Southgate named Harry in his squad for the World Cup qualifier against Scotland and the friendly with Spain in November but didn't feature in either game.

Kane started up front with new Spurs striker Vincent Janssen for the first time against West Ham United on November 19. The game would go down as the first of many classics at White

Hart Lane in the stadium's final season. The Lilywhites came back from trailing 2-1 with just a minute of normal time remaining to win 3-2. Spurs academy product Harry Winks, making his first Premier League start, levelled on 51 minutes after Michail Antonio's header had put the Hammers ahead in the first-half. A Manuel Lanzini penalty saw West Ham regain the lead before Kane's late brace – which included a penalty – won it for the home side.

The ecstasy of the win over West Ham was replaced with the agony of the club's Champions League exit three days later. A 2-1 defeat in Monaco – in which Kane scored from the spot – saw Spurs' hopes of making the knockout phase come to an end. A 3-1 win at Wembley against CSKA Moscow – that saw Harry bag his second European goal of the season – did at least secure the Lilywhites the third spot in Group E and progression to the Europa League.

Spurs were unable to stretch their 12-match unbeaten start to the Premier League season at Stamford Bridge on November 26 as they went down to a 2-1 defeat. Four wins in five in December helped their rise up the table though, as Kane scored twice in a 5-0 victory over Swansea City and was also on target in a 4-1 win at Southampton. He could have easily had a second goal at St Mary's had it not been for an unruly playing surface that affected his run-up to take a penalty which he subsequently blasted over the bar. Harry saw the funny side of that miss, tweeting: "If there's any NFL teams looking for a kicker in the future, have a look at my game tonight!"

In between those wins over Swansea and Southampton, Tottenham also picked up maximum points against Hull City and Burnley in N17 but lost 1-0 at Manchester United. The new year started in impressive fashion as the Lilywhites won 4-1 at Watford, with Kane getting two more goals at Vicarage Road. The win saw Spurs move up to fourth in the table ahead of a match against leaders Chelsea at White Hart Lane.

Throughout the Premier League era, the Blues have been something of a bogey-side for Tottenham. After both clubs were founder members of the division back in 1992 it took Spurs until 2006 to finally register a league win over the west Londoners. Going into the January 4 encounter, the Lilywhites had just four triumphs over Chelsea in the Premier League to their name while the visitors had 26. Despite that record, Tottenham could draw encouragement from the fact White Hart Lane was turning into something of a fortress for them in its 118th and final year. The Lilywhites were unbeaten there during the campaign with eight wins and two draws in all competitions at that point.

On another memorable evening in N17, Spurs were quickest out of the blocks against a Chelsea side looking to secure a Premier League record-breaking 14th consecutive victory. Dele Alli's header in stoppage time at the end of the first-half put the home side in front. Nine minutes into the second period, it was Alli again – with another header – that doubled their advantage. The 2-0 win took Mauricio Pochettino's side to within six points of the Blues.

Kane's first hat-trick of 2017 came on January 14 as Tottenham beat West Bromwich Albion 4-0 at home. It came at the end of a busy week for the England striker who had just become a father for the first-time with the arrival of Ivy Jane Kane. "I've not had many better weeks," Harry told Spurs TV. "It's been a whirlwind of a week, the birth of my daughter, that was incredible, an amazing experience, looking after her all week and then getting ready for this game and to score a hat-trick and win 4-0 in the way we did. It's all been quite surreal really. I don't think it's sunk in yet. The baby is there sleeping at home and I look at her amazed that she's here."

The Lilywhites equalled their club record of six successive Premier League wins with that victory over West Brom and leap-frogged Liverpool into second place in the table. Chelsea – who had been top of the Premier League since a 1-0 win at Middlesbrough on November 20 – were proving difficult to catch at the summit. Spurs drew their next two matches at Manchester City and Sunderland while the Blues won at home to Hull City and drew at Liverpool to extend their lead to nine points.

A Harry Kane penalty secured a 1–0 victory for Tottenham over Middlesbrough at the start of February. A 2–0 defeat at Liverpool the following week saw Chelsea increase their advantage to ten points as they drew at Burnley. With Antonio Conte's Blues in seemingly unstoppable form, thoughts at White Hart Lane turned to the FA Cup and perhaps Spurs' most likely chance of glory in 2017. A second hat-trick from Kane in as many months saw the Lilywhites cruise past Fulham in the fifth round with a 3–0 win at Craven Cottage.

As progress continued in one competition, so Spurs exited another with a 3–2 aggregate defeat to Gent in the Europa League. Over 80,000 supporters packed into Wembley to see the Lilywhites' second leg against the Belgian outfit which finished in a 2–2 draw. The month ended on a real high as Kane made it a hat-trick of hat-tricks for 2017 in a 4-0 victory over Stoke at White Hart Lane – the third successive meeting with the Potters in which Harry's team had won by the same score line.

Pochettino praised his striker – named the Premier League's Player of the Month for February 2017 – after the match. "He's one of the top strikers in the world and I think he deserves it because he's a great professional and top man," said the Spurs manager. "It (the hat-trick) doesn't surprise me, because I've told you many times that for me he's one of the best strikers in the world.

"This season we are not only winning games (at White Hart Lane), we are playing very well here – maybe because we all know it's the last season here and it's a very special atmosphere on the pitch and in the stadium."

Kane's impressive form continued with a brace in Tottenham's next match – a 3-2 home victory over Everton. The forward notched his 18th and 19th Premier League goals that afternoon to head the race for the division's golden boot. He gave Spurs the lead after 20 minutes with a powerful drive from some 20-yards or so. His second on 56 minutes was his 14th goal in 12 league and cup games in the first few months of 2017.

The striker came up against familiar foe in the FA Cup as Tottenham hosted one of his ex-loan sides, Millwall, in a quarter final tie at White Hart Lane. The occasion was soured seven minutes in when Harry sustained an ankle injury in an accidental collision with Lions defender Jake Cooper. He was substituted for Christian Eriksen moments later. In Kane's absence, Spurs went on to win 6–0 with Heung-Min Son scoring a hat-trick. The striker was later seen leaving the ground on crutches and with his right foot in a protective boot. His manager feared a repeat of the injury that kept him out for five Premier League matches and ten club games in all competitions earlier in the season.

"It looks like last time against Sunderland, it was the same ankle," Pochettino told BBC Sport. "We need to assess some more and after tomorrow we will see."

Days later, it was revealed Kane had suffered ligament damage to his right ankle, but it was not thought to be as severe as the aforementioned injury against Sunderland that ruled him out for seven weeks. The striker missed out on the opportunity to be included in the England squad for matches with Germany and Lithuania while he also sat out the next four Premier League fixtures. His Spurs teammates managed to secure a maximum 12 points in his absence.

In true Kane style, he marked his return to the Tottenham line-up with their third goal in a 4-0 thumping of AFC Bournemouth at White Hart Lane on April 15. A good weekend for Spurs got even better the following day as Manchester United beat Chelsea at Old Trafford, with Pochettino's side now just four points behind the Blues ahead of the two sides meeting in an FA Cup semi-final at Wembley.

On April 20, the importance of the game somewhat paled into insignificance when it was reported that Spurs Under-23 coach Ugo Ehiogu had collapsed at the Spurs training ground with a suspected heart attack. The following day, Tottenham Hotspur confirmed the tragic news that the former England international defender had passed away at the age of just 44.

"It is with immense sadness that we announce the passing of Ugo Ehiogu, our Under-23 coach," read a club statement. "Ugo received immediate treatment after suffering a cardiac arrest at the Training Centre yesterday before being transferred to hospital, where he passed away in the early hours of this morning… The Club sends its deepest condolences to Ugo's family."

Kane, like everyone else at Spurs, was rocked by the passing of such a popular figure at Hotspur Way. "Very sad day today! Ugo was a fantastic man and coach! Gone way to soon! Thoughts are with his friends and family now! #RIPUgo" Harry told Twitter.

A minute's applause was observed in memory of Ugo before the Tottenham-Chelsea semi-final – and other fixtures across the country that weekend – as both sets of players wore black armbands. His name was chanted throughout the game with supporters paying their own respects.

On the pitch, Kane cancelled out Willian's early goal with an 18th minute strike. The Lilywhites equalised in the second-half too through Dele Alli, who responded to Willian's penalty just before the break. Goals from Eden Hazard and Nemanja Matic settled the encounter in the Blues favour. After the 4-2 defeat, Harry told the press that the Lilywhites wanted to win the Premier League title in Ugo's honour.

"Ugo was a great character around the training ground, it was just shocking news to be honest," Kane said. "Of course, we'll do everything we can to win the league for him – we wanted to win today for him and for ourselves as well. There are still six tough games left in the Premier League. We can't control what Chelsea do now."

A 1–0 win at Crystal Palace on April 26 – featuring a late Christian Eriksen goal – helped Spurs keep up the pressure on Chelsea as the gap at the top was cut to four points. With the news announced two days later that Tottenham would be their playing home matches at Wembley during the 2017-18 season – hence the current campaign was to be their last at White Hart Lane –– the visit of Arsenal to N17 on April 30 took on extra poignancy.

Rarely will Spurs have enjoyed such a dominant performance in a north London derby as they did that April afternoon. The Lilywhites' 11 shots on target to the Gunners' four only begins to tell the story of their commanding display. And it was Kane, playing in his fifth Premier League meeting with the club whose academy he was once a part of, who led the line. After Dele Alli gave Spurs a deserved lead on 55 minutes, Kane made it two from the penalty spot 180 seconds later. Tottenham fans were able to party like it was 1995 after the game, as the 2–0 victory ensured they would finish above their arch-rivals in the league for the first time since the mid-1990s.

For the second successive season, it was a 1–0 defeat at West Ham United on May 5 that dealt Tottenham's title chances a massive blow. Chelsea's 1–0 triumph at West Bromwich Albion on May 12 saw the Blues crowned champions. Thoughts of that disappointment were cast aside two days later though as the Lilywhites hosted Manchester United in their last-ever match at White Hart Lane. The club branded the occasion 'The Lane, The Finale' and there wasn't a dry eye left in the house that afternoon.

In a beautifully-produced commemorative programme – that was as classy as Tottenham's other arrangements for the day that included a parade of legendary players and a video narrated by Sir Kenneth Branagh – Kane paid his own tribute to the Lane.

"It's great to have been a part of the history here and I've had some special moments at this stadium, even though I've only been playing in it for a few years," he said. "Today's game will be a sad occasion I'm sure, the end of an era. But at the same time, we are now going into an amazing stadium and hopefully the new one will bring even bigger and better memories. I'm proud to have put my mark on the Lane, now I'm hoping I'll make an even bigger impact at the new place."

Victor Wanyama gave Spurs a sixth minute lead in the Lane's curtain call, as the home side's performance lived up to the occasion. Then on 48 minutes, a *Roy of the Rovers* moment arrived as Kane flicked out a leg and made it two. Wayne Rooney got a consolation for Manchester United on 71 minutes, but it is Harry who will forever be remembered as Spurs' last goal scorer at their beloved home.

"No amount of planning for that day could have seen Harry make history by, fittingly, being the last Spurs player to score there," said Spurs TV commentator Daniel Wynne. "The fact we went undefeated at home in the league all season. Wow, just wow. I'm not even going to mention the rainbow at the end of the festivities!"

Liverpool and Leicester City were the only sides who managed to take a point away from White Hart Lane in the stadium's final season. The Lilywhites racked up 20 victories out of 22, including a run of 17 consecutive wins through to the end of the campaign.

Kane's season was the stuff of legend too. His four goals in a 6-1 win at Leicester City on May 18 were followed by a hat-trick at Hull City in a 7–1 triumph on the last day of the campaign. Those goals brought the forward's final tally to 35 strikes in 38 appearances for his club – 29 of those coming in the Premier League. Unsurprisingly, he landed the division's Golden Boot for a second successive season and made the PFA's Premier League Team of the Year for the third time in a row.

The goals kept coming in his final matches of 2016-17, with three strikes in two games for England against Scotland and France.

CHAPTER TEN

RECORD BREAKER

As Tottenham bid farewell to White Hart Lane in May 2017, thoughts turned to the following season when they would be playing their home matches at Wembley. Much was said and written at that time about the club's so-called 'curse' at the national stadium, where the Lilywhites had won just two of eleven competitive matches since the ground re-opened back in 2007.

Asked about Tottenham's temporary move to Wembley after the club's final match at the Lane, Harry Kane offered a positive outlook. "We've got to believe," said the Spurs forward. "I think we had 30-odd thousand (per match) throughout the whole season (at White Hart Lane in 2016–17), we're going to have 80-odd thousand next year (2017–18) so we've got to make that (Wembley) a fortress as well. We finished third last season, second this year – we've got to try and take that next step and try and finish first. Everything is heading in the right direction but we've got to go out there and do it."

Spurs preparations for the season began with a behind-closed-doors friendly against Leyton Orient, while Kane scored a penalty in a 4-2 victory over Paris Saint-Germain in their opening match of the International Champions Cup. The Lilywhites subsequently went down to defeats to Roma and Manchester City during their time at the competition in the United States. The team's first Wembley outing of the season saw them beat Juventus 2–0 on August 5 as Harry and Christian Eriksen netted.

Tottenham's Premier League campaign got underway at Newcastle United, who had won the EFL Championship title the previous season. Following the sending-off of Magpies midfielder Jonjo Shelvey, the game became comfortable for Mauricio Pochettino's side who ran out 2–0 winners thanks to goals from Dele Alli and Ben Davies. The Lilywhites' 2–1 defeat to Chelsea in their first home match of the campaign on August 20 meant talk of the

'Wembley curse' continued. Spurs could draw positives from their performance though. A 1–1 draw with Burnley in HA9 the following week meant their search for a win under the arch went on. In the first three matches, Kane was unable to break an unwanted record of his own – never having scored a senior goal in a competitive match in the calendar month of August.

Kane joked that he "didn't like August anyway" as he tweeted after his two-goal display in England's 4-0 win in Malta on… September 1! Eight days later, it was business as usual in the Premier League as Harry scored twice in Spurs' 3-0 win at Everton. Tottenham's first win at Wembley that season came in their opening UEFA Champions League match in an impressive 3-1 victory over Borussia Dortmund. Pochettino's side had to box clever that evening, with only 32% possession during the 90 minutes. Their clinical edge in front of goal – scoring with three of their four shots on target – was personified by Kane who bagged a brace.

"It's a massive win," Harry told BT Sport. "Nights like this at Wembley, we have to take advantage of it. Last season our downfall was the games at home. It was a more experienced performance from us tonight. In the Champions League you have to be smart. You can't always press teams on a big pitch. We took advantage on the counter-attack and exploited the space they left in behind."

Kane's imperious form continued throughout September. He scored two goals in Tottenham's 3-2 win at West Ham United, got a Champions League hat-trick in a 3-0 triumph at APOEL and netted twice at the Kirkless Stadium, where the north Londoners beat Huddersfield Town 4-0. Unsurprisingly, he was named the Premier League Player of the Month.

In early October, new Manchester City manager Pep Guardiola caused a stir when he gave his opinion on who he thought were the Citizens' main title rivals that season. It wasn't his selection of Chelsea, Manchester United and Spurs that caused the fuss, but his description of the latter simply as "the Harry Kane team". The Spaniard later said he was trying to be complementary to the Spurs striker rather than to belittle his club. "I was never disrespectful to my colleague… I was never disrespectful in a press conference… Never," said Guardiola. "When I talked about Harry Kane's team, it was because Harry Kane was scoring a lot of goals. And I know perfectly that Tottenham are not Harry Kane alone. I think last season, the person who spoke most about appreciating the way Tottenham play was me."

Lilywhites manager Mauricio Pochettino was not impressed though, describing Guardiola's initial comments on Spurs as "sad" and "unnecessary". There is clearly no love lost between the pair, who previously went head-to-head as managers of Catalan rivals Barcelona and Espanyol.

"It's difficult to understand because Pep was part of the big success at Barcelona, when it was Messi at his best. And I never said it was the Messi team. I always said it was Barcelona and it was Pep Guardiola. I think everyone deserves to be recognised as being part of the success of the team.

"I think that many people took his words as very sad and disrespectful to the club. And for many players that are here – it's a strange situation. Personally, I didn't take it in a bad way. It wasn't disrespectful to me. I only express my feeling that, for a lot of people, it was unnecessary to say that.

"We need to move on. For me, Harry Kane is one of the best strikers. It doesn't change anything for me. And I think it's important that our position is (to) be clear, be calm, not be aggressive with our opponent. Our responsibility is massive. But I think it's important to respect every single opinion and I respect his opinion."

Back on the pitch, Harry's late winner for England against Slovenia at Wembley on October 5 saw the Three Lions achieve qualification for the 2018 FIFA World Cup. On his return to club action, Harry was part of the Spurs side that notched their first Premier League win at Wembley as an Eriksen goal saw them down AFC Bournemouth on October 14. Three days later, Tottenham produced a performance of real grit and determination to draw 1-1 with Real Madrid at the Bernabeu. Kane – whose clever run forced Real's Raphael Varane to put through his own net – believed the display was proof the Lilywhites "can handle" playing at the highest level.

"A point at the Bernabeu, you would take that every day of the week. It shows how far we have come as a team," said Kane. "We are happy. Of course, they are going to have chances but we played well and made it tough for them."

On October 20, over 80,000 supporters saw Spurs follow-up their Champions League heroics with a thumping 4-1 victory over Liverpool at Wembley. Kane scored twice in the game, remembered for Dejan Lovren being substituted after 31 minutes of the match as the Reds failed to get to grips with their dynamic opponents. It wasn't a great end to the month for Spurs though. A hamstring injury forced Harry to miss the 3-2 defeat at home to West Ham United in the League Cup and a 1-0 loss at Manchester United in the Premier League.

Pochettino's side topped their Champions League group ahead of Real Madrid's visit to north west London on November 1 and knew a victory over the 12-time European champions would see them through to the knockout phase. Wearing their all-white kit for continental matches – a tradition inspired by their Spanish opponents – Spurs shone under the Wembley floodlights. A Dele Alli brace either side of half-time was followed by a Christian

Eriksen goal that completed a 3-0 victory. The roar from the 83,782 crowd that greeted the full-time whistle almost took the roof off.

If the showing against Madrid was another demonstration of the new and improved Tottenham Hotspur, the 2-0 defeat at Arsenal on November 18 was an unwelcome glimpse of the past. Irrespective of the fact that Shkodran Mustafi's opener for the Gunners probably shouldn't have stood, the Lilywhites were second-best for much of the afternoon.

Luckily for Spurs fans, such disappointments have become rarities in recent times and the team bounced back with an impressive 2-1 win at Borussia Dortmund as the Lilywhites were confirmed as winners of Champions League Group H. "It is massive, an unbelievable night for the fans and the club," said Harry, who scored in the triumph at the Westfalenstadion. "Everyone was doubting us before the group even started that we would not even get through, so a fantastic night.

Kane was also on the scoresheet in the 1-1 draw at home to West Bromwich Albion and the 2-1 away loss at Leicester City that followed. His brace in a 5-1 victory over Stoke City on December 9 was followed by the news he had been named as a contender for the BBC Sports Personality of the Year award for the first time. "It's a huge honour to be nominated," said Harry. "This was always the awards show I remember watching when I was a kid, so to be nominated and be up there with the elite of British sport is fantastic." Mo Farah was that year's eventual SPOTY winner.

2017 ended with Harry setting numerous goal scoring records. He became the first player in Premier League history to score six hat-tricks in a calendar year, while his 39 league goals for Spurs saw him surpass Alan Shearer's total of 36 for Blackburn Rovers set in 1995. Netting 56 times in 52 games in all competitions – including seven goals in seven appearances for England – Harry was Europe's top goal scorer of 2017, breaking the dominance of Lionel Messi and Cristiano Ronaldo in the continental scoring charts of the previous seven years.

He was responsible for half of the hat-tricks scored in the Premier League in 2017 – the others coming from Romelu Lukaku, Joshua King, Sergio Aguero, Alvaro Morata, Callum Wilson and Wayne Rooney. On top of all that, he became the first player to bag consecutive Premier League triples on two separate occasions against Leicester City and Hull City in May and Burnley and Southampton in December. He got eight hat-tricks overall, with triples against Fulham in the FA Cup and APOEL in the Champions League.

A fter the victory over Southampton, Kane spoke of his pride in topping the European scoring charts and his flattery in being compared with the likes of Messi and Ronaldo.

"When you look at Messi and Ronaldo, I've obviously still got a long way to go before I can be compared to them but it's a start and that's what I want to do," he said. "I want to keep improving and be up there one day. That's always the goal, to be bracketed with the best players in the world.

"Messi and Ronaldo have set that standard for so long now. To nick ahead is something I'm proud of and it's just the start for me. I want to do it year in year out. They've done it for eight or nine years now so to be classed in that bracket that's what I've got to do. That's my aim."

Kane's first goals of 2018 came as he netted twice in a 3-0 FA Cup victory over AFC Wimbledon on January 7. It was the start of a four-game scoring run for the striker, who bagged a brace in a 4-0 win over Everton and got Spurs' goals in their 1-1 draws at Southampton in the Premier League and Newport County in the FA Cup. His second in their win over the Toffees saw Harry become Tottenham Hotspur's top goal scorer of the Premier League era, surpassing Teddy Sheringham's record of 97 strikes.

"To be ahead of Teddy is amazing, especially considering I have not been playing in the Premier League that long," said Kane after the victory over Everton. "Teddy was a big hero of mine growing up. It is something I am very proud of but onto the next one... keep winning games and, hopefully, I will keep scoring. Let's just keep adding to it and see how many we can get."

Kane's Spurs beat Manchester United in their last match in January as they consolidated their fifth-place position in the Premier League with the club's top-four aim just two points off. The 2-2 draw between Liverpool and Tottenham Hotspur in February gave rise to a rivalry between the two sets of supporters. With the match tied at one-a-piece with six minutes remaining, Kane appeared to be tripped by Reds goalkeeper Loris Karius and referee Jonathan Moss awarded a penalty. Liverpool manager Jurgen Klopp raged after the game that Harry was in an offside position prior to the spot-kick being given while some fans at the Kop end accused the England striker of diving. From a Merseyside perspective at least, Karius' save from the resulting kick was justice done.

A fine individual goal from Mohamed Salah looked like giving Liverpool all three points in injury time before Spurs were awarded a second penalty – this time for a foul by Virgil van Dijk on Erik Lamela. Again, Klopp and the Anfield faithful claimed they had been hard done by. Kane was in no mood to feel sorry for them as he smashed home his 100th Premier League goal from the spot.

"Both were a penalty and it is not controversial," said Pochettino, offering Tottenham's take on the two penalty awards on an eventful afternoon at Anfield. "Sometimes people complain about the referee, but when they are right it is good to tell everyone."

Kane meanwhile spoke of his relief at slotting home the penalty that earned Tottenham a point in the fifth-minute of stoppage time, having missed one earlier on. "I was nervous before the second penalty," he commented. "It was a big moment, with a lot of pressure, but I stuck to the routine. There was a lot of pressure, in front of the Kop. The first one, I did everything I wanted to and the keeper made the save. You've got to take the chances. I thought the second one was a penalty; the defender took out Lamela."

In the weeks and months that followed, the fall-out from the game continued on social media. It's clear both sets of fans now have an extra reason to want to claim a victory whenever these two sides go head-to-head.

Taking of clubs Spurs love to beat, Arsenal were the visitors to Wembley six days later as the Lilywhites looked to atone for their disappointing display at the Emirates earlier in the campaign. Harry Kane's towering header early in the second-half allowed Tottenham to do just that, as he gave his team a 1-0 victory in a game that saw them have 18 shots to the Gunners' six, while Wenger's men managed just one shot on target. The match was watched by a crowd of 83,222 – the largest-ever attendance for a north London derby and the biggest-ever Premier League turnout. The bumper figure fell just 38 short of the all-time English league record attendance of 83,260 – held by Manchester United for a match against Arsenal in 1948.

Inside the opening ten minutes of Tottenham's Champions League visit to Juventus on February 13, the Lilywhites found themselves 2-0 down, as Argentinian striker Gonzalo Higuain scored twice for the 'old lady' of Italian football. Kane spearheaded an impressive comeback, forcing a save from goalkeeping legend Gianluigi Buffon before rounding him minutes later to reduce the arrears. Higuain's penalty miss for Juve was a huge moment in the match just before half-time and the comeback was complete when Christian Eriksen placed a low free-kick past Buffon in the second-half.

"We could have done [capitulated], away from home in the Champions League – it showed character," Kane said. "It was an excellent performance after that and we take two away goals to Wembley. Great result. I should have scored the header but you have to be ready for the next one and I finished it off."

Harry came off the bench to score in a 2-2 draw at Rochdale in the FA Cup a few days later – Spurs subsequently won the fifth round replay 6–1 at Wembley. He also got the only goal of the game as the Lilywhites triumphed at Crystal Palace on February 25 to move into the Premier League's top four.

Tottenham's biggest crowd of the season – 84,010 – attended the club's round of 16, second leg tie against Juventus at Wembley on March 7. While the Italians were the fastest starters in Turin, Spurs were the better of the two sides in the first 45 minutes in north west London. Heung-Min Son's strike six minutes from the break had the Lilywhites supporters dreaming of a first quarter-final appearance since 2011. But their hearts were broken by two quick-fire strikes from Higuain and Paulo Dybala in the second-half. Not even Harry Kane could save them this time, as his header in the dying moments hit the post and was cleared off the Bianconeri goal-line.

In Spurs' 4–1 win at AFC Bournemouth four days later, Harry limped off after his right ankle was trapped between the legs of Cherries goalkeeper Asmir Begovic. Tottenham subsequently revealed: "preliminary assessments have confirmed that Kane has damaged lateral ligaments in his right ankle. He is expected to return to first-team training next month." The striker was ruled out of Gareth Southgate's England squad for the upcoming friendly fixtures with the Netherlands and Italy, while he was side-lined for the Lilywhites' FA cup quarter-final victory at Swansea City and their memorable 3-1 triumph at Chelsea.

Kane returned to Spurs' line-up at Stoke City on April 7. After a quiet first-half at the bet365 Stadium, Christian Eriksen put the Lilywhites in front early in the second period. Mame Biram

Diouf equalised after a mistake by keeper Hugo Lloris before a free-kick from Eriksen led to Tottenham re-establishing the lead. There was confusion at the time as to whether the ball had crossed the Potters goal-line directly from the Dane's shot or whether Kane had got a touch to beat Stoke goalkeeper Jack Butland.

The goal was awarded to Eriksen at the time but later credited to Kane after a review by the Premier League's Match Centre. "It was my goal, and I rightly claimed it," Kane said. "It was down to the Premier League to make a decision and they did." Eriksen was more than happy for Kane to have been given the goal and said: "Harry celebrated like it was his goal so I will have to take his word for it." The striker meanwhile "swore on his daughter's life" that he got the final touch.

The aforementioned Tottenham-Liverpool rivalry was re-awoken on social media after Kane was credited with the goal at Stoke, as Reds supporters in particular seemed unhappy with the re-awarding of the strike. Harry's effort in the Potteries was his 25th Premier League goal at that stage of the season – four behind Liverpool's Salah, who led the race for the division's Golden Boot. The kind of comments directed at Kane – not just from Liverpool fans – on Twitter regarding the incident ranged from comical to tedious to outright vile. Former striker Les Ferdinand, who scored 184 league goals during his career, said he wasn't surprised at the "over-reaction" to the whole episode.

"After he claimed the goal against Stoke, we saw the world we live in now where a load of people on social media who have no idea about football can give their opinion and totally disrespect somebody never having been in that arena," said Ferdinand. "Harry, like any professional striker worth their weight in salt, who knew he got a touch on the ball, then of course he was going to claim it. As a striker there were a number of occasions in my career where I'd score a goal and other people were telling me I hadn't got a touch and I'd be telling them I had."

Harry offered a similar take to Ferdinand over the flack he took: "Maybe that is the world we live in," he said. "A lot of stuff gets over analysed on social media, but I claimed the goal, got the goal and moved on."

Kane's next Spurs goals came in a 1-1 draw at Brighton & Hove Albion and a 2-0 triumph over Watford. Sandwiched in between was the Lilywhites' second successive FA Cup semi-final appearance in as many years. Tottenham went down to a 2-1 defeat to Manchester United on April 21 despite having led through an early Dele Alli goal. The result sealed Tottenham's eighth consecutive loss at the semi-final stage of the competition – an unwanted tournament record.

After the defeat to United, the FA Cup's official account tweeted Chris Smalling: "What's that in your pocket, Chris?" with a link to an unrelated video of the Red Devils' defender saying: "Harry Kane." The tweet was later deleted and the Football Association issued an apology – not before Kane's boss Mauricio Pochettino had branded the game's governing body an "embarrassment" over the incident.

A few weeks later, when asked to comment on the social media message, Kane added: "The FA tweet was a silly tweet. We all know that. I talked to the gaffer (Pochettino) about it and all we said was: 'Would other countries do that to their players?' Probably not.

"It is something that has gone. Two weeks ago, now or whatever – I am over it. The gaffer may have said I am sad but I am focused. I am a guy that gets over things. If it happened, it happened. I move on and look forward to the next game and that is all I worry about.

"Maybe it's a mentality thing. It is easier nowadays maybe to banter England players or take the mickey out of the England players. So, if we don't do well in the World Cup, then they can write and say: 'We told you so.' But that is maybe a weaker mentality.

"It is what it is. We are focusing on what we have got to do. We have got to go with the mindset and belief we can do it. We try to win everything we go into. The World Cup is no different."

The disappointment of another trophy-less season for the club – the Lilywhites hadn't won one since their League Cup triumph of 2008 – was tempered with a third successive Champions League qualification. This was sealed with a 1-0 win, and a Harry Kane goal of course, against Newcastle United on May 9. Four days later, Spurs ended the season with a 5-4 victory over Leicester that included two more strikes from the club's golden boy and ensured a third place finish in the Premier League. Harry ended the campaign having scored 30 goals in 37 Premier League matches and 41 goals in 48 matches for the club overall.

Harry's 30 strikes during the Premier League season were directly responsible for adding 22 points to Spurs' tally – the greatest impact of any player to their club in the division. Mohamed Salah was second on that list, with his 32 strikes bringing Liverpool 16 points while Burnley's Chris Wood was third with his ten goals contributing 12 points. Despite this, Kane missed out on the division's Golden Boot, which went to Salah while the Egyptian also won the PFA Player of the Year award. Harry was included in the PFA Premier League Team of the Year for a fourth consecutive season.

Despite Kane's obvious commitment and dedication to his boyhood club, Spurs supporters always have the worry in the back of their mind that their 'crown jewel' might one day depart for the prestige, glamour and riches of a Barcelona or Real Madrid. As the striker was captaining England at the World Cup during the summer of 2018 though, they could rest easy. Their beloved son had just put pen-to-paper on a new contract shortly before flying off to Russia, committing himself to the club until 2024.

"I'm really excited, it's a proud day," said Kane on signing the new deal. "Obviously it's been a great few seasons and I'm looking forward to the future. It's been fantastic to consistently get in the Champions League so I'm really excited to have another go at that and with the Premier League and FA Cup, we'll look to go as far as we can. For us as a Club, it's just about keeping improving and we'll work hard to do that."

CHAPTER ELEVEN

OFF THE PITCH

Once upon a time, a six-year-old named Oscar Loukianos wrote a letter to Harry Kane. He invited the Tottenham striker to his house to "play football at 4pm on Friday". Harry replied, telling Oscar he couldn't make it as he had a big match of his own. He asked Oscar if he fancied coming to watch his 'kickabout' instead? England versus Estonia at Wembley Stadium, starting at 7:45pm. Don't be late. Harry played and England won. After the match, Harry invited Oscar to come and meet him and they talked about their favourite team, Spurs. It was a footballing fairy tale that ended happily ever after.

And so, another heart-warming story about Harry Kane – an individual who those who know him best have described as "a normal bloke", "down to earth" and "a perfect role model". Chris Ramsey, who coached the striker from under-12 level right the way up to Tottenham's first-team has his own tale to tell about Kane.

"In the run-up to this summer's (2018) World Cup, I won an award for services to youth development," explained Ramsey – who was the recipient of the Eamonn Dolan Award – for innovation and exceptional contribution to football coaching and coach development over the past season – at the 2018 Premier League Youth Conference Awards Dinner.

"Having been presented with the award, a video came on the screen with a message of congratulations that Harry had recorded for me. Given his commitments at that time, with a World Cup coming up and given his global status in the game, it was an amazing thing for him to do. I was pretty choked up, not least because a host of other players recorded their own messages too including Tom Carroll, Ryan Mason, William Troost-Ekong…

"That's what Harry's like though. He's one of the best players in the world, but he always spends the time to keep in touch with the people he has met along his football journey. If you text him, he texts you back. I think he remembers the people that had faith in him."

The Spanish football title *Marca* offered their own take on Kane's character, having interviewed the Spurs striker in 2017, describing him as "sensible, measured and prudent."

"He plays golf in his spare time, he doesn't drink alcohol, he doesn't go clubbing; that is the life of Harry Kane," added writer Lorena Gonzalez. To what extent those statements are true, only those in Harry's inner circle will know. What is clear is that despite being a global sporting superstar, playing in the richest football league in the world, it's rare for him to be cast into the media spotlight for anything other than his performances on the pitch.

His limited public profile – relatively speaking – and apparent level-headedness is even more incredible when you consider that at the age of 24, Kane signed a six-year-contract with Tottenham Hotspur worth an estimated £62.4m. His basic salary is said to be £200k-a-week plus bonuses. While never coming across as the type to be overly concerned with material possessions, Harry has still enjoyed the trappings of success – and why not?! His family home in Essex comes complete with a swimming pool and a cinema-cum-golf-simulator room while he owns a second property close to the Spurs training ground in Enfield, where he will sometimes stay during the week. His car collection has included a £99k Land Rover Autobiography, a £200k Continental GT Supersports and a Jaguar F-PACE.

"I pretty much love that Jag," Kane told *The Sun Motors*. "It's not too big, not too small, it fits our little daughter and the dogs. It's a family car with a sporty edge. It's not like you're embarrassed to drive it as a dad. You're happy to drive it. It looks nice and it's not too expensive. It's been great for me so far."

One of Kane's undoubted passions away from the football pitch is golf. In an interview with *Express.co.uk*, the Tottenham striker described the sport as his "biggest weakness". "Whenever I can get the time, I'll go to the course for a game," he said. "It's probably not the best for my relationship as I don't actually get many days off."

Harry has been playing since the age of 16 and had whittled his handicap down to four at the time of writing. He regularly posts images of himself out on the fairways and his most frequented local courses include Abridge Golf Club and Woolston Manor Golf and Country Club while he shot his first-ever level par round at the Centurion in May 2015. The list of world-renowned courses he has played across the world includes the Liberty National in the United States, Baker's Bay in the Bahamas as well as Kingsbarns and St Andrews Links in Scotland.

When asked in that same interview with *Express.co.uk* what would be his perfect way to spend a Sunday in addition to "having an early game of golf," Kane added: "Going for a long walk with my family and two Labradors. Then I'd come home, have a barbecue and watch the NFL and the golf."

One of Kane's dogs – introduced into their household in October 2014 – reflects another of Harry's great sporting interests – American football. Brady is named after NFL legend Tom Brady but Harry has rubbished reports that Brady's brother and the Kane's other dog Wilson was so-called after fellow quarterback Russell Wilson. "My fiancée named hers Wilson," confirmed Kane to *NFL Films*. "It was the same year that Patriots played the (Seattle) Seahawks in Super Bowl, so everyone assumed it was for that reason but it wasn't."

Having started watching NFL with his fiancée's brother, Harry became a keen follower of the New England Patriots and

Tom Brady in particular, who he credits as inspiring his own football career: "The lowest moment (of my career) was probably when I was at Leicester City, and I just couldn't seem to get into the team," wrote Kane in his essay for *The Players' Tribune* "They were still in the Championship at the time — and I just remember sitting in my flat and having this terrible realisation of, like, 'If I can't play for Leicester in the Championship ... how am I supposed to play for Spurs in the Premier League?'

"A few weeks later, I was sitting in my flat again — and at the time I was really getting into the NFL. If I wasn't training, then I was playing *Madden* or watching New England Patriots videos on YouTube. So one day, I happened to stumble on this documentary on Tom Brady. And it's all about the six quarterbacks who were taken before him in the NFL draft. Turns out, Tom Brady was the 199th pick in his draft class. Imagine that. It just blew my mind — but in a good way. The film really struck a chord with me."

Kane has attended NFL games in the UK in the past including the Kansas City Chiefs-Detroit Lions clash at Wembley in 2015. With Tottenham Hotspur having agreed a ten-year contract to stage a minimum of two NFL fixtures a season at their new stadium, Harry will doubtless be watching a lot more gridiron in person in the near future.

For all his sporting passions, the biggest love of Harry Kane's life is of course his fiancée Katie Goodland. The pair first met when they attended Chingford Foundation School and later started dating in 2012. Katie is a sports science graduate and a personal trainer. "She (Katie) always wanted to do her own thing," said Kane of his bride-to-be in an interview with *Esquire*. "She went to university and worked hard."

The pair got engaged on July 1, 2017 during a holiday to the Bahamas, when the England captain proposed on the golden sand of the Caribbean archipelago. It was quite a year for the young couple, who'd celebrated the birth of their first child – Ivy Jane Kane – on January 8, 2017. "I thought it would be harder but she is sleeping OK," said Kane on his early days of parenting in an interview with the *Daily Mail*. "Sometimes it's a bit surreal. I pick her up and can't quite believe that she is really mine. But I am changing nappies and all that. No problem." The Kanes' second child was due around the time this book was released in August 2018.

In his interview with *Esquire*, Harry admitted adjusting to life in the public eye had been a "little crazy" for the couple, who got together at the age of 18. "We went to school together, so she's seen my whole career," added Kane. "Of course, she's finding it (the public interest in the couple) a little crazy. I think she's even been in the papers a couple of times taking the dogs out.

"If I was single now and meeting people, you'd never know if they were with you for the right reasons. Is it the money? You'd never really know. So, I'm lucky that I've got a childhood sweetheart."

The pair have kept their wedding plans under wraps to date and given Harry's reluctance to talk about his private life in any great depth in the media, it's fair to assume it will stay like that all the way up to the big day.

Unlike many of his teammates, Harry doesn't have any tattoos on the advice of his father, who told him he would "regret it when I get older". His unfussy, slicked back hair, with short back and sides has long been his signature look and his dress sense can be defined as classic rather than bling-bling. "Blazer and a shirt, that's my sort of style," Kane told *Esquire*. Fully aware of the perception some Premier League players have of being idle and somewhat over-paid fashion victims, the Tottenham striker is proud to have steered clear of that image. "A lot of footballers get stereotyped now," he told *The Sun*. "A lot of them get tattoos, a lot of them get dodgy haircuts. The fact I was clean-cut, an Englishman with slicked-back hair who was just going out and working hard, I think people kind of took to that. I think they could appreciate it."

During the World Cup, Harry was joined in Russia by his parents Pat and Kim and older brother Charlie. After Kane's hat-trick in the 6-1 win over Panama, the family met up in Nizhny Novgorod and posed for a photograph together with the match ball. That same day, Katie celebrated her baby shower in a tepee in the garden of the couple's Chigwell home where a big screen was set-up for visitors to watch the game. The tent was also decked out with flags of St George and a poster of Kane with 'he's one of our own' emblazoned across it.

Harry's performances at the World Cup saw him awarded with the freedom of his home borough – Waltham Forest. He was born in Whipps Cross Hospital, raised in Walthamstow and schooled in Chingford. Clare Coghill, Waltham Forest Council leader commented: "Harry Kane is a hero to millions but it isn't just his footballing ability that marks him out to be given the freedom of the borough.

"He has shown incredible perseverance and maturity throughout his career and to be captain of England at a World Cup at the age of 24 shows just how much leadership qualities he possesses. I'm proud that our borough welcomed his Irish father, that his family could make their home here, and he received the opportunities to make the most of his footballing talent.

"Whilst the World Cup had to come to an end – sadly one game earlier than we all hoped – our men's football team gave us much to be proud of this summer."

Such was the interest in the England captain in the run-up to Russia 2018 and during the tournament itself that even individuals that looked like the Tottenham man found themselves in the news. Harry Kane lookalike Dan Milligan was interviewed by Newcastle's *ChronicleLive* during the World Cup as was fellow doppelganger Danny McLaughlin on ITV's *Lorraine* show. Having tweeted a photograph of himself to Kane in June 2017 with the message "If I had a £1 for everytime (sic) someone said you look like a chubby @ HKane I would be as rich as you pal," Middlesbrough's Paul Foden claims to be the 'original' lookalike.

"A few years ago, I remember my auntie mentioning I have a resemblance to Harry," said Foden – aka Chubby Harry Kane – whose day job sees him drives refuse collection vehicles for Redcar and Cleveland Council. "I don't really see it but more and more people started to comment in pubs and on the street so I just went along with it. When I tweeted saying I looked like a chubby Harry Kane, I got something like 3,000 likes and over 1,000 re-tweets.

"I can remember a song starting up for me in a pub on a drunken night, referencing my likeness to Kane. Since then, I've probably had over 150 requests for selfies. After my tweet went viral, *The Sportsman* got in touch asking me to pop to Manchester to do a World Cup music video with (Martin) Bell and (Johnny) Spurling and (Neil) 'Razor' Ruddock. It was just a bit of dancing and a few video clips of myself celebrating and scoring penalties. Then Bell and Spurling gave my name to Andy Harmer who runs the lookalikes.co.uk agency and I got signed up. I got asked to attend Atlantic Records' World Cup Party for the England-Belgium game to meet and greet people, have selfies taken etc. I did the same for the England-Sweden game, travelling to a pub in Manchester for *The Sportsman*.

"Andy deals with the finances but I get between £400 and £500 as a fee for lookalike work, although when I have worked with *The Sportsman* I have just asked for travel expenses and food and drink.

I don't really demand anything I am more up for great memories and if I can take the wife then bonus!"

While some make a living out of looking like him, the real Harry Kane is doing pretty nicely when it comes to his own business interests. The England captain trademarked the phrase "HK Harry Kane" and a logo with the government's Intellectual Property Office in relation to particular goods and services including 'clothing', 'games and playthings' as well as the 'providing of training'. The trademark is something the player could licence in the future or use as a means of endorsing certain items. Christano Ronaldo for example has trademarked both 'CR7' and 'CR9' and previously had his own range of 'CR7' Nike products.

Kane currently has his own sponsorship deal with the sportswear giants Nike and wears their Hypervenom boots. In celebration of the player scoring his 100th Premier League goal against Liverpool in February 2018, a special-edition boot – the Nike Hypervenom 3 HK – was launched. The boots – coloured blue and white for Spurs – feature a golden swoosh and the number '100' on the heels, insoles bearing the message "KEEP IT KANE" and his surname on the tips of the laces. During the World Cup, he starred in an advert for headphone brand Beats by Dre called 'Be Defiant' – having also been a part of their commercial activity around UEFA Euro 2016.

In the run-up to the World Cup, sponsorship consultant Nigel Currie told the media that Kane has the ability to double his estimated £10m-a-year basic contract at Spurs through endorsements. "If Harry stays fit he could be earning £10m-a-year for five or six years," said Currie, who added; "Tiger Woods earned 70 per cent of his money away from the golf tournaments." With tie-ins with the likes of Mars, Lucozade Sport, BT Sports and Hugo Boss Parfums in addition to Nike and Beats by Dre, Harry is as smart off the pitch as he is on it.

For someone who, by his own admission "can't remember the last time I went to a (night) club", Kane's biggest 'showbiz' moment to date came when he presented Kendrick Lamar with the 'Best International Male Solo Artist' at the 2018 Brit Awards with Camila Cabello. The former Fifth Harmony member obviously enjoyed meeting Harry, as she filmed herself supporting England and singing 'he's one of our own' in tribute to the striker during the World Cup.

Comedian and Arsenal supporter Jack Whitehall introduced Harry onto the stage at the Brit Awards by saying: "Our next presenter is a Tottenham striker... meaning the Brit award he hands out tonight will probably be the only trophy he gets his hands on this season." Spurs teammate Dele Alli ended up having the last laugh though. In an episode of *Training Days*, Whitehall commented to Alli "I think Harry Kane might hate me quite a lot," to which the midfielder replied, "I don't think he knows who you are... just saying!"

Calvin Harris was one of few Scotsmen to be delighted with something that Kane did at Russia 2018. After scoring his hat-trick against Panama, Kane was asked to name a song he'd use to celebrate his triple. After giving it some thought – he answered: "I'll go 'One Kiss' by Calvin Harris and Dua Lipa." "Yes I'm Scottish but I don't care the legend Harry Kane picked our song," posted Harris on Twitter, with a clip of the post-match press conference.

A keen player of video games, Kane streamed his online *Fortnite* battles with Tottenham teammate Alli shortly before heading to Russia. Jan Vertonghen, Toby Alderweireld, Michel Vorm, Eric Dier and Kieran Tripper are amongst the other known gamers in the ranks at Spurs. Harry plays EA Sports' FIFA series too and was named in the Team of the Year in *FIFA 18*, joining Lionel Messi and Cristiano Ronaldo upfront.

During the World Cup, Trippier paid a glowing tribute to Kane when asked what makes him so special. "It's his character, his personality, I see that on a day-to-day basis," Trippier replied. "He dedicates his life to football. He's so professional. He's the first one in, the last one out every single day we're in. He looks after himself, doesn't drink alcohol or anything."

The striker's focus in terms of keeping himself in peak physical condition appears to know no bounds. At an England press conference in October 2017, Kane revealed how ice baths, stretches and a personal chef are all factors that help him feel "as fresh as you can be".

"I think, over the last year or so now, I've changed a lot off the pitch with the nutrition side of it," he said. "It kind of clicked in my head that a football career is so short. It goes so quickly, you have to make every day count.

"So, I have a chef at home to eat the right food, helping recovery. You can't train as hard as you'd like when you have so many games, so you have to make the little gains elsewhere, like with food. That will help me going into a tournament year, with my body and my recovery."

"I was always eating well, never badly. But I have a guy come round and he explained what you could do, eating the right food at the right times. You could eat healthily all week and then carbs before a game, and that could make your body go into shock because you're not used to it. So, maybe higher carbs sometimes, lower other times, making plans around training. I started doing that on January 1 (2017) – a New Year resolution.

"I met the guy in December (2016). I spoke to him and it blew me away a bit. I'd never looked too much into it, but when he explained what the body does and how he could help me recover... He helped me in the recovery from the (ankle ligament) injury (sustained v

Sunderland in September 2016), with certain foods I was eating. It opened my eyes a bit.

"He's there (at Kane's home) every day, Monday to Saturday, and leaves it in the fridge for Sunday. I hardly ever see him because I'm at training, but he'll cook the food and leave it in the fridge. We've got a good plan going and it seems to be working."

"When you're playing Saturday, Wednesday, Saturday, there's not a lot of time to train, so it's about making those little gains in other ways: ice baths, stretching, nutrition... that keeps you as fresh as you can be. It's a big part of football nowadays. Other players are doing the same thing. My career has gone so quick already, I want to make the most of it."

When speaking to *Fitter Happier* back in 2015, Kane said his guilty food pleasure is "the odd bar of chocolate". He also admitted to the *Express* that despite his healthy lifestyle he "likes bad food" and added: "I always crave the unhealthy stuff but have to keep myself in check, particularly during the season. There will always be times when you have bad things – I love pizza or steak and chips. But it's important for me to perform at my best, so I only really do it as a treat when I've had a good game or gone out with the family for a celebration."

Kane has previously taken cookery lessons and has said his signature dish is a chicken paella. Remembering back to the days he studied catering with Harry, school friend Luke Robinson told ITV's *Lorraine* during the World Cup that the Tottenham man is as a dab-hand in kitchen;

"(Harry) loves catering, he was actually really good at it as well," he said. "We had catering class once a week and we'd have a set meal, go home get the recipe and come back and cook it. He'd always have his Tottenham chef prepare that recipe, so it was healthy and it would help him with his football. But he did have a little secret as well… he loved a crumble, a little apple crumble with the custard. He made a mean apple crumble, I can't lie."

On the occasions he gets to dine out, Kane loves Sheesh in Chigwell – which specialises in Turkish cuisine. The restaurant is run by Dylan Hunt and the building it is located in, the former Ye Olde Kings Head, is owned by ex-Tottenham chairman Lord Alan Sugar. Harry and Lord Sugar have been pictured there together in the past. The pair also teamed up to help raise over £50,000 for Comic Relief in 2017, as part of a challenge to silence the tabloid big-gob and Arsenal fan Piers Morgan on Twitter for a day and to force him to wear a Spurs shirt. "I'll donate to help reach the @comicrelief target," Kane tweeted Sugar. "I'll double my contribution if @ PiersMorgan kisses the Spurs badge on live TV."

Kane supports a number of charities including Noah's Ark Children's Hospice – a community-based hospice service providing support for children and young people with life-limiting or life-threatening conditions and their families in north and central London and Hertsmere. Harry visited the home of 13-year-old Joe – who has a life-limiting condition – and his family during National Volunteers Week in 2015. He performed household chores such as ironing, gardening and making tea as well as having a kickabout with Joe and his brothers Nate and Fran in the back garden.

Joe's parents Anna and Andrew sent a message to Kane during the World Cup which read: "We are all delighted to see Harry doing so well in Russia and wish him and all the team the best of luck – he really is one of our own."

Since 2007, England players have donated not only their international match fees but also their time to good causes via the England Footballers' Foundation (EFF). Before the World Cup kick-off, the EFF had raised over £5m for various charities and provided over 300 player appearances for worthy events.

By qualifying for the knockout phase of the tournament, Kane and co had each raised £54,000 for the Foundation, while the 23-man-squad's subsequent run to the semi-final raised around £4m collectively.

One of the charities EFF has donated funds and player appearances to is Honeypot – established in 1996 to enhance the lives of young carers and vulnerable children aged 5-12 years. Harry and England teammate Andros Townsend visited young carer Charlie Milne as part of EFF's work with Honeypot. "I can just remember him (Kane) being so nice and smiley and cheerful," Milne told *ITV News* during Russia 2018. "He wasn't judgemental at all… he was understanding… he was down to earth and genuine."

The personal tributes to Kane are as plentiful as those praising his attributes as a footballer. "You couldn't hope to meet a nicer lad," said his former manager Harry Redknapp while ex-Wales international Robbie Savage described him as "humble and down-to-earth off the pitch". His current boss Mauricio Pochettino once joked he is so "in love" with Kane that; "now my wife is so jealous – and his wife too." During the World Cup, Harry said of the Argentinian: "Poch texted me… He sent a lot of love hearts and said 'Come on England.' He is rooting for me. He is not just my boss; he is my mate. He is the manager, but he is a friend as well."

The bromance between Pochettino and Kane is music to the ears of Tottenham Hotspur supporters.

CHAPTER TWELVE

A BRIGHT FUTURE

The immediate – and Spurs fans will hope, long term – future for Harry Kane will see him playing his club football at the new, £850m Tottenham Hotspur Stadium.

The state-of-the-art arena, with a seating capacity of 62,062, is the largest club venue in London and features the biggest single-tier stand in the country, which holds over 17,500 spectators. The on-site microbrewery is a world-first for any stadium as is the dividing, retractable pitch. Premier League or NFL matches – the latter organisation said to have contributed £10m towards the construction of the new ground – can staged there at the touch of a button. The club meanwhile have capitalised on their corporate appeal, with members of the £30k 'Tunnel Club' able to view the players through one-way glass as they prepare to take to the field. The equally swanky 'Sky Lounge' offers panoramic views across the capital.

All being well, Kane will have lined-up for the Lilywhites in their plush new surroundings for their first-ever Premier League match there against Liverpool on September 15, 2018.

The spectacular stadium is a towering symbol of Tottenham Hotspur's rising stature in world football. The Lilywhites were ranked as the 11th richest club in the world in the latest edition of Deloitte's *Football Money League*, with their revenue having increased by £96.4m in a 12-month period – from £209.2m (€279.7m) in 2016 to £305.6m (€355.6m) in 2017. On the pitch, Spurs achieved qualification to the UEFA Champions League for the third-consecutive season in 2018.

A pre-World Cup study by CIES Football Observatory valued Kane as the most expensive footballer on the globe, with its algorithm putting a £176m price tag on the player's head. Neymar – whose world-record £200m transfer from Barcelona to Paris Saint-Germain in 2017 – was valued at £171m while PSG club colleague Kylian Mbappe was third on the list at £163m. Tottenham's Dele

Alli was sixth behind Lionel Messi and Mohammed Salah with a value of £150m.

Financially, the sums add up right now for Spurs and their reported £200k-a-week earner Kane. However, the real barometer of success for both going forward will be reflected on the pitch rather than the balance sheets. Harry was watching from the stands as a 14-year-old fan the last time the club won a trophy – the League Cup in 2008. Silverware is therefore an absolute priority for player and team.

Hopes of a bright future for both were bolstered in May 2018, when Head Coach Mauricio Pochettino – so integral in the rise-and-rise of Spurs and Kane in recent seasons – put pen-to-paper on a new five-year-contract. "I am honoured to have signed a new long-term contract as we approach one of the most significant periods in the club's history and be the manager that will lead this team into our new world-class stadium," said the Argentinian on his new deal with the north Londoners.

Kane signed a new contract of his own during the summer of 2018 as did fellow first-teamers Heung-Min Son, Erik Lamela, Davinson Sanchez and Michel Vorm. Young Irish forward Troy Parrott – who dreams of one day emulating Harry's success in N17 – penned his first professional deal.

The Premier League is the trophy that stands atop of Tottenham and Kane's wish list. The Lilywhites' challenged for the title in both 2015-16 and 2016-17, with Harry firing in the goals, as Pochettino's side came third and second in those respective campaigns. Their third-place finish in 2017-18 was also a significant achievement, given all their 'home' matches were played at Wembley Stadium rather than in N17.

"I think it is bigger than other years," reflected Kane on Spurs' qualification to the Champions League at the end of the 2017-

18 campaign. "I'm really proud of the team and the club, we've worked hard. People underestimate how tough it's been, 38 games away from home in a competitive league is tough especially with the top six all fighting for a Champions League spot.

"The next step is winning stuff but this has been a big year for us and hopefully we can have a massive year next and win some trophies."

When he spoke to Sky Sports at The Open in July 2018, Kane stated his belief that Spurs could challenge current champions Manchester City for the Premier League title. "Yeah of course we can," he said. "We've been up there for the past few years but the Premier League is tough. It doesn't often go like that (that a team wins back-to-back titles)."

While the title is the ultimate goal, qualifying for the Champions League and improving season-on-season will be another key indicator of the progress being made by player and club. "It (the Champions League) is the big attraction," said Kane. "You want to be playing Champions League football and it is important for us with the new stadium. I can't wait for those Champions League nights at the new home. I can't wait to see it all done up for the fans. They remember White Hart Lane as a special place but this place will be absolutely incredible."

"Of course, I have visualised winning the Champions League," said Kane in another interview. "Which footballer hasn't?"

Kane and Tottenham's most realistic chance of a trophy – especially in the immediate future – might come in either the FA Cup or League Cup. They've come close in both competitions in recent years, reaching the FA Cup semi-final in both 2017 and 2018 and were League Cup finalists in 2015. While winning a cup would seem to be lower down on the club and manager's list of priorities, silverware in any form would be welcomed by Spurs supporters and Harry has expressed his affection for both competitions;

"I've always said, just keep progressing, keep getting better. We want to start winning trophies so that's the aim. As long as the club keeps doing that then I'm happy here." The elephant in the room is whether Tottenham can keep Kane and other star players in the event that they remain trophy-less in the next few seasons.

There is no doubt that Harry has a level of loyalty and devotion to Spurs that exceeds most players to have worn the famous Lilywhite shirt over the last decade or so. But with links to European heavyweights including Barcelona, Bayern Munich, Real Madrid, Manchester United and Manchester City, could there ever come a point in his career where the striker contemplates life away from N17 – especially if he remains without a winners' medal?

"It would break the fans heart if he left," Kane's former manager Tim Sherwood told talkSPORT in a 2017 interview. "The last person to come through the club was Ledley King. Harry's a superstar. He will continue to score goals. He's got everything. I hope he stays at Tottenham for the rest of his career... The only danger is that team across the water also in white (Real Madrid)."

Of Kane's possible future suitors, Real Madrid are the most frequently mentioned in dispatches. Luka Modric and Gareth Bale both departed N17 for the Bernabeu during Daniel Levy's chairmanship of Tottenham, who once heralded a "special relationship" with Los Blancos. Madrid themselves have made no secret of their interest in Harry. The Spanish club's former president Ramon Calderon once told *The Sun*: "The (transfer) objective for Real Madrid, no doubt, is Kane. If they want a player for the next five or six years they are going to go for Kane but Levy is going to ask a fortune for him."

There are no shortage of individuals offering an opinion on whether or not Harry should remain with Tottenham until the end of his career. One former Spurs manager Andre Villas-Boas commented: "If he has a hunger for trophies and for notoriety he would have to leave Spurs" while another ex-Lilywhites' boss, Harry Redknapp said: "I don't see why he should leave, he'll be captain eventually, he's loved there."

For the here and now, Kane is most definitely staying put. In July 2018, the player was 1/20 to be a Tottenham player by the time the summer transfer window closed while a move to Real Madrid was a 9/1 shot and 33/1-plus to go to any other club. Ex-striker Dimitar Berbatov told *Betfair*: "I don't see Kane leaving for Real Madrid, not at this current moment. The club will have a new stadium soon which shows ambition to him and the squad is building on top of their foundation. He'll stay and fight for silverware for now, but further in the future, I cannot be sure."

But what of the player himself? Where does Harry Kane see his long-term future? Thankfully for Spurs supporters, there have been many suggestions from the England captain that he could remain with the Lilywhites for the rest of his career.

"My goal is to play my entire career only for Tottenham," Kane told German newspaper *Bild am Sonntag* in 2017. "We have a fantastic team, a great coach, a professional training centre and we're getting a new stadium. At the moment, everything suits me here and I'm happy."

"If you want to be a big club then you have to keep your big players and I love it here," Kane said in other interview with the *Daily Mail*. "I work for one of the best managers in the world and have one of the best young teams in the world, so why leave?

"Some players want to earn as much as possible but for me it is about being happy. Money is a plus to what I do but it doesn't make you happy on its own. Now it's time to turn that into winning something. We have talked about it but really need to do it."

He also alluded to his affections for Spurs and the club's place in his long-term focus in his essay for *The Players' Tribune.*

"I dreamed of playing for Spurs since I was a boy," he wrote. "For a long time my motivation was simply to close my eyes and picture myself scoring against Arsenal in the Premier League. (I've) Done that a few times now, and it never gets old. But now, my motivation is a bit different. Now, I close my eyes and I picture myself lifting the Premier League trophy at our new stadium with my mates. I'd trade the next 100 goals for that feeling.

"We've been close the past few seasons, but there's only one way to close the gap – and I'm afraid it's quite a boring answer. As my dad would say, we've gotta keep working, keep doing. Keep getting on with it."

If he remains a Tottenham player for the entirety of his career, a major target for Kane – other than winning trophies – would be to break Jimmy Greaves' all-time club record of 266 goals. The striker has previously been asked whether he could surpass Greaves' Spurs tally to which he replied: "Of course. I always set my targets a bit smaller, maybe month by month every couple of months, but if I carry on the way I am going then, hopefully, yes."

Asked whether he thinks Kane will break Greaves' Spurs scoring record, Harry Redknapp commented: "Tottenham have got a great chance to achieve big things. They have an outstanding group of young players there and Harry is the leader of the team, the top man. I can see him being the club's leading goal scorer for many seasons to come and he's got every chance to break Jimmy Greaves' all-time scoring record for the club long-term."

Prior to the start of the 2018-19 season, Kane stood 22nd on the Premier League's list of all-time, top goal scorers with 108 strikes. He should move up quite a few places in the near future, with Jermain Defoe and Sergio Aguero the only players above him on the list still playing in the division. Harry was just a goal behind Manchester United legend Ryan Giggs' total of 109, five behind ex-Arsenal forward Ian Wright and 38 off his boyhood idol Teddy Sheringham who is tenth currently.

Les Ferdinand – who is ninth, having scored 149 Premier League goals for the likes of Queens Park Rangers, Newcastle United, Tottenham Hotspur, West Ham United, Leicester City and Bolton Wanderers – believes Harry is capable of topping Alan Shearer's all-time record of 260 goals in the division during his career. "If he can avoid any major injuries, he looks like being the first striker in a long while with a real chance of doing just that," said Ferdinand. "He has the capability to join the 200 club (occupied by just Shearer and Wayne Rooney) for sure."

Kane is clearly driven by goal scoring targets and has previously admitted he would "love" to break Shearer's record. "One day, who knows, I might even be able to go for Alan's 260 goals in the Premier League," commented Harry. "You dream about those things but for me wins are more important than personal records."

Another tally in Kane's sights is Wayne Rooney's 53 strikes for England, that makes him the leading goal scorer in the history of the national team currently. Harry played and scored the night Rooney broke Sir Bobby Charlton's record of 49 goals for the Three Lions, as he converted a penalty in a 2-0 home triumph over Switzerland. The Croxteth-born forward increased his tally with strikes against France, Australia and Iceland before retiring from international football in August 2017.

Kane's six goals at Russia 2018 took his senior England record to 19 strikes in 30 appearances at the age of 24. By his 30th cap, Rooney – aged 20 at the time – had 11 international goals. The Manchester United and Everton legend averaged 4.2 goals a year over the next decade to eventually reach his tally. If Harry were to play and score for England at the same rate as Rooney going forward, he would need to be in the team at the age of 34 to break his record. His next strike for the Three Lions will take him level with his former teammate Jermain Defoe and 1966 World Cup winner Martin Peters on 20 goals.

When he was quizzed about the possibility of breaking Rooney's record back in 2015, Kane said: "It's just about doing what I can for now and doing things right, trying to score as many goals as possible. Maybe in ten years we'll see where I'm at. Hopefully still playing for England and still playing at a high level."

Rooney meanwhile has spoken highly of Kane and hailed him as "the best striker in Europe right now," in the run-up to Russia 2018. "It hurts him when he doesn't win, and you can't say that about all the players. He really wants to win and score goals, he wants to improve. He is the natural leader now in that England team. He is the one that really has to wear the armband."

Kane has previously said that he would "swap 100 goals" to win a trophy with Tottenham and the striker would surely pass-up the opportunity to be England's record goal scorer if it meant he could win a major competition with the Three Lions. The next chance for Gareth Southgate's team to claim their first notable piece of silverware since 1966 comes in the shape of UEFA Euro 2020 – subject to qualification of course. England are paired with Spain and Croatia in the newly formatted UEFA Nations League A Group 4, which will part-determine their route to the European Championships.

In recognition of the 60th anniversary of the tournament, UEFA decided to host fixtures in 12 cites in 12 countries across the continent as opposed to single or duel nations staging the competition as has previously been the case. For Kane and England, the prospect of both semi-finals and the final being staged on home soil is a tantalising one. Whether or not Harry will get to lift the Henri Delaunay trophy on July 12, 2020 at Wembley, who knows? Two years prior to the competition, the bookmakers made England a 10/1 shot for Euro glory while world champions France were 5/1 favourites.

Kane will undoubtedly be one of the most recognisable figures at the tournament, as long as he and England get there. His standing in the global game was reflected in July 2018 when he made the ten-man shortlist for *The Best* FIFA Men's player award alongside the likes of Cristiano Ronaldo, Lionel Messi, Luka Modric, Antoine Griezmann, Kylian Mbappe and Mohamed Salah. Gareth Southgate was amongst *The Best* FIFA Coach of the Year nominations.

Harry will surely be included in the list for the 2018 Ballon d'Or too. Pre-World Cup, he was 66/1 to land the prize, but his odds dropped to 10/1 after the tournament. If he were to win it, Harry would be the first Englishman since Michael Owen in 2001 to be named as the world's best footballer. Five-time winner Cristiano Ronaldo is 1/5 favourite to collect a record-sixth award in 2018 though.

Longer-term, the World Cup will next be staged in 2022 in Qatar, by which time Kane will be 29. The tournament – the last to involve 32 teams before it is increased to 48 – will be the first to be held outside the traditional months of May, June and July. Instead, action will get under way in the Western Asian state on November 21 with the final being held on Qatar National Day on December 18.

The scheduling of the tournament provides a major conflict with top leagues around Europe, including the Premier League and its usual busy pre-Christmas fixture list, not to mention the Champions League, which has matches in November and December. In England, the top division may well kick-off a month early in July 2022 with a slight extension to the end of the season also being planned to accommodate the World Cup. If Kane and England both appear at Qatar 2022, dealing with the effects of a busy 2022-23 season will surely be a welcome problem.

The make-up of the England team by 2022 will obviously be different to the one we see today but is also likely to include a nucleus of players from Gareth Southgate's side that reached the World Cup semi-final in 2018. The Three Lions have enjoyed a number of major successes at youth level in recent years, winning both the Under-17 and Under-20 World Cup in 2017. Could Kane be paired up front with Rhian Brewster – who was the Golden Boot winner in England's success in the Under-17 tournament with eight goals – in Qatar? Will Under-20 captain, Lewis Cook, be a regular in midfield by then? Only time will tell.

In an interview with Sky Sports in 2018, Kane expressed his desire to be "a consistent goal scorer for the next ten years." "My dreams are to stay at a consistent high level for the next seven, eight, nine years," he continued. "I want to keep myself in good shape, play for a long time. I think that is what makes a good player, doing it year in, year out, if you can catch records that's amazing, I don't think of that but it comes along the way.

"Every day a thought forms in my head that I want to win a trophy, how good it would be to win the FA Cup this year, or the Premier League next year, or the World Cup... that's definitely what I want to achieve." When quizzed by *ESPN Brazil*, Kane touched on the fragility of a career in professional football. "For me, a football career is so short, I'm going to do everything I can in a short period of time to achieve what I want," he added.

Right here, right now – and putting the talk of trophies, awards and records to one side – one of most important things for Kane is to keep enjoying his football. The passion the striker carries for the beautiful game is obvious. "You come in, you train, you play, you go home, you rest... that's kind of a footballer's life... I love doing it," Harry once reflected. From kickabouts with his dad and brother at Ridgeway Park in Chingford as a six-year-old to playing at a World Cup aged 24, it seems the striker rarely feels as at home as he does with a ball at his feet or as elated as he does firing a shot into the back of the net. "I always loved the feeling of scoring," confirmed Kane to Sky Sports.

The satisfaction Kane gains from his career is replicated by the happiness he brings to his many fans. As Tottenham supporter Crackers described him: "Harry is every one of us in the stands that's doing it on the pitch... And boy is he doing it."

"Harry Kane's appeal to me is two-fold," continued Crackers. "Firstly, he is an incredibly gifted striker who has pushed himself into the category of world class. This has come via a combination of natural ability but more importantly his sheer bloody-minded determination to improve and push himself every day, week, month, tournament, season etc. Secondly, this world class player still to this day feels like just an ordinary lad that grew up supporting Spurs and then went on to make it."

Fellow Spurs supporter Mike Leigh echoes Crackers' sentiment on Tottenham's favourite son:

"Harry Kane emerged just when we really needed a new terrace hero – the fact that he was a local boy and Spurs fan made it even sweeter. To many he seemed like he would be another home grown that wouldn't quite make the grade and disappear. Showing enthusiasm but not having that final quality to truly make it. Fans of a certain age can look back at the always willing but limited

(Chris) Jones, (Gerry) Armstrong, (Ian) Moores, (Mark) Falco, (Paul) Walsh, (Chris) Armstrong and (Roberto) Soldado. They all tried their best in a Spurs shirt but were not the top quality that we craved like (Garth) Crooks and (Steve) Archibald, (Gary) Lineker or (Jurgen) Klinsmann.

"What we have with Harry is someone who is – as records already show – up there with the (Jimmy) Greaves, (Martin) Chivers, (Jermain) Defoe and (Alan) Gilzeans. One can argue he has more attributes than some of them. For a fan base that has always looked back so fondly on – let's be honest – not enough great memories in 50 years, we finally have someone who can lead this team to the very top again. He may look like a throwback player from the 60's with his swept back short back and sides, but he is truly a great modern player. Disciplined, hungry for goals, and like us all is desperate to win things for his beloved Spurs."

Kane's performances at Russia 2018 cemented his place as England's footballing golden boy. While every player will have their detractors at international level, the majority of Three Lions followers realise the ability, the determination and promise the Spurs man brings to Gareth Southgate's team.

"It's easy to forget the media pressure on an England captain – endless interviews and being the face of the team," said Mark Heelis, who cheered Kane and the Three Lions on from the stands at the World Cup. "Harry didn't let the captain's responsibilities wear heavy on him like it has previous captains. He appeared honoured, pleased to grasp the opportunity and savour every moment. There is no over confidence or getting carried away with Harry – he was a fitting captain – calm, intelligent, astute, inspiring and a team player.

"Kane and many other players will return from the World Cup better for their experience, more mature, with confidence that yes we can compete in the latter stages of a major tournament. The future is bright for these young lions and there is a lot to get excited about. The buzz around England is back and with games at Euro 2020 being held at Wembley including the final what better time for football to come home."

At 25 – and with so much achieved already – you still get the feeling Harry Kane's footballing adventure is only just getting started. His legendary status at Tottenham Hotspur has long since been confirmed, his value to the England national team he captains is obvious. Over the next decade though, the boy from Chingford has everything in his armoury to propel him to the level of the game's true greats.